Raising Ryan

Living with Autism

Kimberly Reeves

Ryan Cunningham

Published by
TSKAdventures Press
Bellingham, Washington

ISBN-13: 978-0692104514 (Kimberly Reeves)

ISBN-10: 0692104518

Printed in the United States of America
Set in Garamond
Original text designed and formatted by Ryan Cunningham
Publisher Logo designed by Ryan Cunningham

Cover photo: Kimberly Reeves
Authors' photo: Jessica Olson jessicaolsonphotography.com

For

Dad

Table of Contents

Acknowledgements   vii

Foreword   xiii

Introduction   1

Living With Autism   7

The Journey Begins   11

Uh-oh Houston, We Have a Problem   15

What's In a Word(s)   25

Acceptance   33

Public School: Part I   39

And Then There Was Music   45

Widowed   55

Public School Part II   63

You Got This Ry   75

On The Edge   87

In His Own Words   97

Shaving   107

Seizures and Surfing   115

Electronics   125

Too Many Puzzle Pieces   133

Problem Solving   149

Pegasus   159

Happy Birthday to You   165

Baby Steps   175

Legal-ease   183

Inclusion   191

A Swing and a Miss   201

A Hole In My Heart   207

Parting Thoughts   217

Acknowledgements

Raising Ryan began as a story to myself, a recounting of the experiences I had as a parent rearing my son alone. My writings were meant to heal my sadness and to provide closure to my perceived losses in regards to Ryan's future and independence as an adult. I never once considered that my series of short stories, retellings, could morph into anything that resembled a book. But, with the extraordinary support and constant, not so subtle nudges from my family and friends, I began to believe and trust that maybe, just maybe, they were correct.

There is a laundry list of people that helped make this project a reality. My parents, never faltering in their support, always believing that I had a story worth telling and that my protagonist was the most incredible young man that any grandparents could hope for. My sister Laura, for telling me over and over again how this book was going to make a difference for families of autistic children and to keep writing. I want to thank my community of friends that provided me with constant support and positive feedback, knowing that Ryan's story needed to be told and convincing me that I was the one to do it. To my editors, Dana Weaver, April Varn Cope, Clare

Jones, Malora Christensen, Michael Lacher and Ellen Creagh, I want to thank them for stepping up to the plate and generously giving of their time with absolute enthusiasm. Without their keen eye, this book would have gone to press with more than a few blunders and I am grateful that they were willing to comb through and find my missteps.

There are multitudes of people that gave freely of themselves, helping Ry to meet his potential. Without their love, support, dogged determination and openness to Ry's differences, I cannot imagine "who" Ryan would be today. Rick Anderson and Ellen Van Houten, Ryan's Instructional Assistants, were my lifeline to hope while Ry struggled through his first 8 years of public school. They provided consistent and loving care of my trusty sidekick and became members of our family. Finding the right words to describe how much they have meant to Ry and me doesn't seem possible. Thank you is not enough.

And finally, I want to thank my trusty sidekick and co-author Ryan. I cannot imagine the person I would be without him in my life. I am forever blessed that he was born to me and continues to teach me what it means to live life to the fullest. He is my emotional compass, my inspiration - he awes me with his ability to embrace his differences and with his bravery to face challenges head on.

~KCR

There's a long list of people without which my life could not be as it is—Jay Alexander, my neurologist at Seattle Children's Hospital; Charles Cowan, the director of Seattle Children's Autism Center at the time of my diagnosis of autism in 2004; and Stephanie Wallace, my geneticist, also at Seattle Children's Hospital.

Let me also not forget Joan Ganz Cooney and Lloyd Morrisett, founders of Sesame Workshop; and Stacey Gordon, the actress performing Julia on *Sesame Street* (Sesame Workshop's flagship show). *Sesame Street* has done a very good job in making all autistic people around the world feel like they are welcome in a world where they have been so frequently excluded.

Thanks to all of you.

~RCC

Today you are you!

That is truer than true!

There is no one alive who is you-er than you!

Theodor Seuss Geisel

Foreword

As both a pediatrician and a father of twin boys with
autism, I read, with great interest, the memoir by Kim
Reeves, *Raising Ryan*. The experiences of having a child, or
in my family's case, two children with autism, were all too
familiar to me, and were realistically conveyed by Ms.
Reeves' narrative. Beginning with the hopes and dreams
we instill in our newborn children, particularly in the
author's case, as she had suffered through previous
miscarriages. And then the slowly progressive, sinking
feeling, despite no previous or professional experience in
child development, that something is wrong with your
child. The maze of doctors, specialists and testing, hoping
for reassurance, but knowing full well how it is going to
end. And then, once confronted by the diagnosis of
autism, the need to face a long road of interventions,
treatments, understaffed and overburdened schools and
teachers, well intended as they may be, and the
bureaucratic nightmares, all in the anguished process of
trying to get your child the best care possible. And having
to relive the grief of the diagnosis with every form filed
out, every health history given to a health professional,
every defensive and embarrassed explanation to a staring
parent, while your child falls to the ground in the middle

of the grocery store in a raging tantrum. Finally, the need to ignore your own anxiety and grief, gathering all the strength you can to be your child's advocate and make them the best they can hope to be.

All of this is detailed in *Raising Ryan* in a chronology that, although painfully familiar to any parent with a disabled child, contains insights unique to Ryan and Ms. Reeves that explore the heartache and heightened responsibility that autism imposes on all parents. Principle among them being the observation that even with the laser focus we all must have on our disabled children to ensure their success, life still goes on all around us, as it does for all families. There are jobs to go to, relatives to deal with, and all the myriad of quotidian activities that now must find room in an overwhelmed life. In Ms. Reeves' case, that other life was in itself a source of amazing stress. The death of her husband, Ryan's father, from cancer, the added medical issues of Ryan's seizures (as if autism wasn't enough for both of them to handle) and the need for emergent brain surgery when Ryan injured his head.

But, what struck me as the most compelling aspect of the story was that, despite the endless hits to normality that Ryan and Ms. Reeves endured, there was a consistent tone of optimism that coursed throughout the book. This included taking advantage of any promising sign from Ryan, including his attraction and seemingly inborn talent for music, and his penchant for electronics. Especially entertaining and interesting to read was Ms. Reeves' desire to expose Ryan to all varieties of activities - even skiing - never giving in to autism's isolating force. This, combined with her intense and persistent curiosity to discern how Ryan's mind saw and interpreted the world around him, was inspiring and should serve as a testament to the tenacious love of a mother for her child.

Joseph Zibulewsky, M.D., M.H.S., F.A.C.E.P., F.A.A.P.

Introduction

There is a remarkable Mystery that slowly unfolds with the birth of each child, each grandchild.

Ryan Campbell Cunningham is certainly his very own unique one-of-a-kind human being, yet we two - Grandson and maternal grandmother - share certain genetic traits that clearly identify us as related.

For example: Ry and I see most events in our life contextually- from the inside out. This perspective creates for us indisputable "facts", that when presenting our case, others would argue are subjective and irrational, but for us, these multilayered perceptions are both real and irrefutable. Ryan as a preschooler would tell you that the cement in the courtyard at his mother's college was pluses and exxes. While he could not describe the tiles without the significant details of the grouting pattern, he also could not recognize the entirety of his mother's face. His processing only allowed him to discern a portion at a time, making it dangerous for them to get separated by even a few feet in a strange place. Trying logically to convince Ry that the cement is just a sidewalk or that his Mother is simply across the room could not stem the deluge of emotion that overtook our dear boy like a tsunami as he desperately fought to realign his world into a recognizable place of safety and security.

Autism, as unique as the human who has it, makes many of Ry's descriptions or reactions inexplicable. His mother, my daughter, realized her task was not to teach Ryan to live solely in her world, but to first understand his. As an adult who attempts this, I can tell you it is more difficult than learning a foreign language or a complex math skill.

Most grandmothers enjoy bragging rights when there is a new baby in the family. I don't know about other cultures, but here in the United States, we love comparisons. From the earliest days of pregnancy, the expectant mother reports her progress and compares "notes" with other mothers. This soon becomes a steady social competition that lasts throughout our lives; who does what earliest, or first, or best. Parents and grandparents of autistic children develop caution about sharing their child's accomplishments. The often atypical nature of their child's progress or lack of development makes membership in this circle of exchange awkward and often unbelievable. In Ryan's second year a friend asked me if Ryan was beginning to be interested in reading from watching a popular children's show. Her two year old was. How to honestly and casually share that Ryan was spontaneously reading chapter books some of which were his mother's anatomy texts? With our remarkable Ryan we soon learned that his advanced achievement in one area usually highlighted his equally as remarkable deficit in another. Who knew that the day would come when I would pray that Ryan be gifted with less savant-like intellectual ability and more "common sense" to smooth his way into daily living.

Taking care of Ryan while his mom recovered from her C-section I spontaneously sang an Australian ditty over and over to sooth his colic.

Kooka Burra sits in the old gum tree
Merry, merry king of the bush is he
Laugh Kooka Burra
Laugh Kooka Burra
Gay your life must be.

At the time I mused, wondering what the words were telling me about this tiny lad. Was there a prediction of a childhood filled with laughter or perhaps a future of travel abroad? Maybe a same gender relationship? I was left with a feeling that Ryan had an unusual lifetime ahead - one foreign to me. And so he has. No matter how many articles, experts, or other parents the caregivers of an autistic child consult, there are no answers, no guarantees, no explanations for the soul-searching "whys".

Does anyone ever pause and wonder how the parents of special needs children continue to love and nurture their child (and in some families, children) in spite of the extreme fatigue, the intense anxiety, and the ever-dwindling hope? In the early days I watched Ryan as he scripted, rapidly walking the same repetitious route through the house speaking out loud to no one in particular. His behavior appeared intimately significant, which Ryan would fiercely repeat if interrupted. Yet it made no sense to me. It was difficult to find the tiniest connection between us.

Even today as Ryan, now a high school graduate, comes across country for an annual visit and declares my house is his other home. There are so many gifts of connection we share, yet I know that as much as he yearns to be "normative", he at age eighteen struggles to learn independent living skills and cannot recognize me if he were to meet me away from the familiar setting of this home.

It takes a village to rear a child to adulthood. It takes vastly more with autistic children because adulthood eludes them and their childhood often outlasts the village. This book is written honestly, compassionately, informatively and most importantly as a guide to assist parents, teachers, and the helping profession recognize that autism is a community concern. Rearing an autistic child takes courage, a keen sense of humor, a reservoir of tolerance, many, many mentors and a determination to cultivate the humanity in each and every special needs person.

I have four grandchildren and four great-grandchildren. Each of them has offered me their own baby versions of gifts. Ryan sat at the piano at age two and played a song following the notes that he perceived were represented by the colors of the M&Ms he had lined up across the music stand. When I asked him the name of his melody he said, "*My grandma song*." Today he gifts me with describing a very complex philosophical question or by correcting a computer dilemma. In many ways Ryan does "live" in a foreign land and we, who love him, join him and celebrate when he chooses to join us where we live. Together, these two worlds are slowly blending, offering hope and possibility for all the special needs persons who are marginalized, rejected, or neglected because of their differences.

As a grandparent, educator and therapist, this book has been an education for me. May it be for all who read it. I have such respect and care for both the special needs individual and all who participate in assisting with their care. May your lives be blessed with unexpected support and love.

Paula M. Reeves, Ph.D.
Author of *Heart Sense* and *Women's Intuition*

Living with Autism

By Ryan Cunningham

To have autism has been a wonder for me. Though autism does have some side effects, my life has been generally positive, and I have felt very happy and safe.

In my first grade at Sunnyland Elementary, a girl (whose name I would rather not disclose) bullied and probably harassed me out on the playground. She was high up on the step-bars, and I was on the floor. She had done (and would continue to do) the same thing to nearly every other student she would meet. I do not know what else motivated her to bully me. Luckily, no one else bullied me since then.

I have since learned to control my outbursts, and to stay calm and not be as grouchy[1] as I sometimes was back then.

That led me later to be very welcomed in the choir program at Squalicum High School directed by Andrew Marshall and later by Jason Parker. I had perfect pitch (in

---

[1] Referencing Oscar the Grouch from *Sesame Street*.

other words, if you, the reader, played a 440 Hz pitch for me, I could immediately tell it was an A natural).

I have also learned computer coding, including by working from home with Sugar Labs[2] to report and sometimes fix bugs in their software. They all welcomed my contributions.

I am also discovering that *Sesame Street's* Muppet, Julia (also discussed elsewhere in this book) has taught me that people with autism really deserve respect. This only furthers the message that "it takes a village to raise a child."

With everything there is and has been to support me, I feel just so welcome in this world.

However, I have unfortunately been too inactive in advocating for myself.

---

[2] Sugar Labs is a member of the non-profit Software Freedom Conservancy, which develops software to share in One Laptop per Child's mission of distributing computers in low-income countries.

To have seen Julia from *Sesame Street* - finally, a Muppet[3] that represents autistic people like me - is just amazing.[4] It is even more amazing to be in a community that welcomes and accepts me for who I am, instead of denying me for who I am not. (Some months ago, I made a small donation to the Autistic Self-Advocacy Network [ASAN] and named in my honor Stacey Gordon, who plays Julia.)

I am just so empathetic, caring, and loving, and generally care for others very well. It very much hurts me for someone to say I am retarded. It even hurts me for someone to say to someone else (in my vicinity) that the other person is deaf-mute, dumb, lame, or possessed by the Devil merely because of his or her disability (though I do not practice religion).

Speaking of that, my self-determination class at Community Transitions[5], two days ago, engaged in a

---

[3] The Muppets are a puppet franchise created by Jane and Jim Henson in 1955 for the television show *Sam and Friends*. They have since made their way to other TV shows, including *Sesame Street* and *The Muppet Show*.

[4] I am paraphrasing Sesame Workshop's own words.

[5] Community Transitions is a life and work skills program for 18- to 20-year-olds in Bellingham School District No. 501 (Bellingham, Washington, USA).

Spread the Word to End the Word rally at Western Washington University. (For the uninitiated, Spread the Word to End the Word is a campaign organized in a partnership between Special Olympics and Best Buddies to end use of the word *retard* and its derivative forms in reference to those with intellectual disabilities.) While there, I held up a poster and also sang one song from episode 4715 of *Sesame Street* (where Julia premiered) and another from *Les Misérables* ("Do You Hear the People Sing?").

In the past year, I have begun advocating for myself by telling others I needed extra time to process my thoughts, and in a few cases by asking for help navigating a steep hill (because I have some gravitational insecurity). I believe that advocating for oneself and others is very important whether or not you have a disability.

The Journey Begins

My son, Ryan, is autistic. Actually, his extensive medical file describes him as high functioning autism with seizure disorder, Chiari malformation type 1, vitiligo, macrocephaly, irritable bowel, hyper mobile joints, low muscle tone and presents like Sotos Syndrome. That's a mental mouthful! I describe him as a highly intuitive, empathic, linguist, techie, gifted pianist Buddha boy that wants to open his own Spanish language school for children and author children's books.

Ry came into this world ahead of my maternal schedule but perfectly aligned with the obstetrician's. You see my son decided to turn bum down in my 32nd week of pregnancy. The doctors wanted to flip him but I refused. No one was gonna mess with this boy! The year before, I had lost a pregnancy in the seventh month and I was not taking chances with this child. I was thirty four, had been pregnant four times and this little boy could sit in my uterus however long he seemed fit. So with that declaration, my Frank breech baby with a 38mm head was abruptly brought into this world three weeks ahead of schedule.

My first thoughts, lying on the operating table as Ryan was placed into my arms, were thankfulness that he was finally here and that he was healthy; a vulnerable, knee-buckling take-your-breath-away love that I had never experienced. And fear. *I am a parent... what now... how do I do this... what if I screw up?* I want to believe that every first time parent can agree with my thoughts and experiences.

There was nothing remarkable about this newborn, except the fact that he was mine, beautiful and perfect. But as babies go, he pooped, peed and threw up on me with uncanny consistency, had gas-bubble smiles, colic, cried and slept. He seemed to be progressing. He found his toes, next his thumb, rolled over, and sat up; the usual cuteness of a little person. It wasn't until he was six months old that things began to shift ever so slightly. I vividly recall him sitting in his swing, his head turned to the left, looking out of the upstairs window for prolonged periods of time. I remember thinking that it must have been the dappled sunlight playing through the trees capturing his attention. It never occurred to me that it might be something more than that. I was new to parenting and did not know this level of focus was unusual. I let it go and continued through new parent bliss.

At his sixth month well-baby check up, his pediatrician asked me a battery of questions. *Does he point to objects he wants? Can he track a moving object? Is he sitting up with frequency and trying to crawl?* With each question I answered' "*no, not yet*!" It didn't occur to me that these things should be happening with frequency, all children develop at different rates. But his doctor felt differently and said she was going to keep a closer eye on my boy. Frankly, I was on board with that strategy too.

Over the next few months, paying more attention, I began to notice more and more behaviors that were becoming worrisome. Case in point: I have a colleague who is a great guy, incredibly animated and wonderfully quirky and insightful. We have been teaching science side-by-side for twenty-five years and we know each other well. So when I had Ry, Steve was thrilled for me. One day, like any other day, I had Ryan with me at work. His nine-month-old wonderfulness was tucked away in the sling I was wearing over my left shoulder, with just his eyes peeking over the edges. As Steve approached us, he began dancing around, making silly faces and sounds, trying to engage my son. Initially, I thought Ryan would recoil from the stimuli, shy and turning his head away from Steve , but he didn't. He did nothing. Actually, absolutely nothing, as I looked down at my child, I saw a hundred mile stare passing straight through Steve. At that instance I turned to my friend, Jeanne and said, *"I wonder if he is autistic?"*

That's a horrible place to be as a parent - suddenly questioning the health and well being of your child. As quickly as I made the statement, I erased the thought from my mind. No way, not him, not my son...he is perfect!

This is the beginning of Ry's story - the process of recording my experiences raising an autistic child on my own. The uncertainty, fear, grief, sadness and most importantly the joy needs to be shared, if only with myself while I write.

Uh-oh Houston, We Have a Problem

Months before Ry's third birthday, his father, Lee, was
diagnosed with metastatic lung cancer - non-curative,
palliative care... prognosis, three to six months. Fuck! Up
to that point, Lee, retired, had been a stay at home dad,
Ry's primary caretaker. I was nine years into a teaching
career I adored and was eager to continue working.

The first months of Lee's diagnosis were a whirlwind of
tests, surgery, radiation, chemo and exhaustion. In
desperation I called my mother, admitted that I was not
Wonder Woman, and asked, *"Please, I need your help, will you
come?"*

She promptly closed her practice and made a beeline to
Washington State to help us through this tenuous period.
Mom's primary charge was Ryan...

While Lee slept or disappeared from us with another trip
to the hospital, Mom rolled up her proverbial sleeves, dug
in and helped me raise my son while I finished up my
spring quarter teaching responsibilities.

One day, just home from work, Mom relayed her day with Ry, the sandbox and sticks. You see, Ryan loved the sandbox that Lee made for him. He would sit for hours, filling measuring cups and watching the sand pour out, back and forth, forth and back; therefore, it was not surprising that he and his grandmother had spent a pleasant May afternoon playing at the sand box. But her story took a left turn from the ordinary.

As was their routine, my mother would put Ry in his Radio Flyer wagon each day and schlep up and down the driveway for an hour or so looking at flowers, rocks and whatnot. This particular day, Ry was interested in small twigs, green with new sap. As they walked, they collected. Their day's journey ended at the sandbox...blissful rest for Mother's tired legs and Ry's outdoors safe play space.

At this point in life, Ry was already repeating the alphabet and I thought nothing of it. I had no idea when that occurred in the development of toddlers, but it seemed like a natural activity for Ry because it came so easily to him. I soon found out how wrong I was in that assumption.

Anyways, back to the sand box. While playing in the sand, Ry grabbed his green sticks and started to bend them into shapes. As Paula, my mother, recounts the story, it took a short period of time before she realized that her grandson was creating the letters of the alphabet. Here was her beautiful tow-headed two-year-old grandson fashioning letters out of sticks they had collected on their wagon adventure.

As I sat on the love seat listening to her, half of my brain was thinking, yep, that's my Ry guy. The other half was scared and wondering what was going on. I can't remember if Mom offered any insight that day, but I immediately reflected back to the first time she held Ry.

Shortly after he was born and I was recovering from my C-section, Mother came to Washington to help, eager to get her hands on her fourth grandchild. As she walked into the door, I held him out to her. With tears forming, she cradled him and quietly said, *"Something's wrong"*. Her words were not meant to upset me...well, too late for that...but she is wildly intuitive and couldn't help herself. Also, she and I have a relationship based upon communication and she trusted that I would receive her words with the knowledge that it was meant to reflect a loving and caring concern. In addition, within minutes she was hesitantly and painfully telling me that my cousin

Steve, a S.W.A.T. Captain, had been gunned down in the line of duty. Her comment about Ry took a backseat as I sat there in shock trying to wrap my head around the loss of my "twin" cousin.

So, once again, I filed away the stick incident to the incredible life of Ry, the wunderkind - no harm, no foul. I had no idea what was in store over the course of the next year.

When I reflect back to that time, there were four pivotal moments that shifted me from curious observer to panicked parent in hyper-drive.

Event 1: Coca-Cola cans meet Ry
My husband Lee did not drink Coke, he consumed it at a rate that would astound and amaze most casual by-standers. On a light day, he would cruise through a 6 pack with three to four coffees as a chaser. On a bad day he had a twelve to sixteen can habit. I was buying twelve packs of Coke as if my life depended on it. One day, while unloading groceries from the car, a twelve pack broke apart in the kitchen, cans skittering every which way. Ry toddled into the kitchen and began to build a pyramid. I thought how cute, Coke building blocks. As he was

constructing his red and white creation I began to notice the spacing between the cans. Ry was putting together this pyramid fairly quickly. He wasn't spending a lot of time assessing and never once did he change the placement of a single can. As I said, I noticed something unusual. The cans seemed to be spaced apart equally. It was so uncanny that I ran to the shop to get a measuring tape and sure as shooting, every can was 1.25 inches apart - exactly! When he finished building, I took apart the pyramid and he began again. This time he was placing them into a French curve and yes, every can was 1.25 inches apart. I was amazed and it began to niggle at my brain to pay more attention.

Event 2: The Ball Pit

A couple of weeks later, I had Ry at a local children's play space called Tube Time. There were tunnels, slides, bouncy rooms, ball pits and what sounded like a hoard of toddlers and small children screaming their way through a fantastical time. Ry was quiet and took in the scene. It was his first time here and he had never experienced this degree of bedlam. As I looked around I saw that a ball pit was unoccupied - perfect. I grabbed Ry's hand and we were off to conquer this corner of kiddie heaven. Now, you would think my son would jump around and throw balls this way and that - you would think! Nope, not a chance! He quietly moved towards the center of the pit and began to sort the balls by color. Blue in this corner, red over there, green behind him and he wanted yellow close by. He had been doing this for a few minutes when his activity was interrupted by a few little people and their watchful parents. The children entered the pit and did what kids do. All the while, Ry continued to sort. As I stood and watched, a mother came up to me and asked what my child was doing. I looked at her blankly, because, well, it was obvious that he was sorting. I smiled and said he was playing. She looked at him, looked back at me and said, *"What's wrong with him?"* WHAT'S WRONG WITH HIM?! Can you imagine the look on my face? I held my tongue, which was a monumental task, promptly grabbed my son and, as he started to cry, whisked him away.

Event 3: Look Mom I Can Read

Two weeks before Ry's third birthday we were sitting together on the deck, Ry on my lap and a children's white board in front of us. Initially we were drawing silly stick figures of this and that. Suddenly, I decided to play a word game with him. At the top of the board I wrote *at*. Next I wrote and sounded out the letter *m* and then added *at...mat*. Then *cat*, *sat*, *bat*...you get the drift. Next up was *it*. I wrote and sounded out the letter *s*, added the *it* and Ry looked at me and said *sit*. What? Okay kid here is an *m*. He said *mitt*! What was going on? My not quite three- year- old son was reading or decoding words - this is not possible.

I was a young reader, but I knew this was not normal, average or an anomaly. We played for another fifteen minutes or so and then I was on the phone to my mother. She confirmed my belief. *" No Kimberly, that is not normal."* Now what? I felt immobilized with the next steps. I had a very sick husband I was caring for and a toddler that was reading and shouldn't be.

I distinctly remember coming home from work a couple of months later. Ry was in the great room on his belly looking through my anatomy textbook. As I walked up to him, he looked me squarely in the eyes and asked, *" What is sarcoplasmic reticulum?"* What three year old asks that? My three year old does.

Event 4: I Think I Need a Timeout
Not long after the sarcoplasmic reticulum event, Ryan began to retreat. My bubbly, always giggling toddler was slowly disappearing within himself. He stopped making eye contact, basically stopped talking, became rigid and started

having real tantrums. Not terrible twos quality scream fests - my little guy was running through the house and throwing himself at walls. And really who could blame him? His primary caretaker was *in absentia*. In the past 5 months Lee was a ghost in the house or stationed at the hospital. In essence, Ry had lost the most central person in his life, his father. I thought Ry was lashing out and grieving. And in retrospect that was partially true, but was no way near the entire story.

You would think that all of these events would have gotten me into motion. At this time very few people were talking about autism and very little was known. Temple Grandin had not gained her popularity yet and autism was not a garden-variety word.

At the time of Lee's diagnosis, I was lucky enough to work for a college that had an on-campus child development center and blessedly, the director, Ray Soriano, bent all the rules to make a space for Ryan.

One day while picking Ryan up from the center, my colleague and acquaintance, Ray, pulled me into his office and confirmed my fears. He was quite certain that Ry was autistic and needed an evaluation. I can't tell you how angry I was and fired off at Ray with both barrels... how dare he... what did he know... I grabbed Ry and stormed out of the building. Why was I angry at Ray? He was doing what was best practices and professionally sound. He knew early intervention would be key to Ry's development and success. I was angry because I was afraid, scared, and devastated that this could be true. Now what?!

What's in a Word(s)

Autistic Disorder:

1. Impairment in social interaction:

> a. impairment in nonverbal behavior such as eye to eye gaze, body, posture, facial expression, and gestures to regulate social interaction - check!
>
> b. failure to develop peer relationships - check!
>
> c. lack of social or emotional reciprocity - check!

2. Impairment in communication:

> a. delay in, or total lack of , the development of spoken language - nope!
>
> b. with speech, impairment to initiate or sustain a conversation - check!
>
> c. lack of varied, spontaneous make believe play -

check!

3. Restricted, repetitive behaviors and interests:

> a. restricted behaviors or interests abnormal in intensity or focus - check!
>
> b. repetitive motor mannerisms (hand flapping, etc.) - check!
>
> c. persistent preoccupations with parts of objects -

nope!

Ry hadn't been diagnosed yet and, in fact, I had not even gotten an appointment with his pediatrician for confirmation. But I did get my hands on a copy of the *Diagnostic and Statistical Manual for Mental Disorders* and it was daunting! There was this "spectrum" of disorders with behaviors that seemed hard to navigate. Did Ry have Asperger's? How about Pervasive Developmental Disorder Not Otherwise Specified? Fragile X? Maybe it is Autistic Disorder? Argh! Time to see his doctor.

Ry's pediatrician at the time, Nancy Bischoff, had been keeping a watchful eye on his development. Every parent will attest that the well-baby checks are essential and mind-numbingly frequent. Basically, the baby was weighed, measured (length, head circumference), given a shot or three, while parent filled out questionnaire and chit-chatted with the doctor about baby. Any questions? No? He is doing great. See you in a few weeks!

My kiddo was always in the upper 90th percentile in weight, length and his head circumference was off the scale - he had a big head (macrocephaly)!

For most of the developmental milestones, Ry did okay. He was slow to sit, crawl and walk, but within the norms.

What he didn't do was track an object when it was dropped or point to items he wanted, and that got Nancy's attention. As stated in chapter 2, she was keeping a watchful eye on my son.

When she saw his abrupt changes in the winter of 2003, she knew that he needed an assessment and recommended and referred us to the University of Washington's Autism Clinic in Seattle. Good! I was finally going to get some answers, but not without a lot of work and helpful intervention.

At the time, I lived in a smallish, rural town, with no traffic lights and most folks knew each other by name or pick-up truck. Imagine Mayberry with lots of dairy cows, raspberry farms, and rain, nestled in the foothills of the upper left coast of the U.S. We lived about three miles, as the crow flies, from the Canadian border. It's the kind of town that doesn't allow for secrets and neighbors unite when there is a brutal nor'easter in the winter or too many garden zucchini and tomatoes in the summer.

I was struggling to get an appointment at the U.W. clinic. In fact, I couldn't get anyone to pick up the phone. Call after call and I was on a first name basis with the answering machine, but never received a call back. I suppose the front office was having issues at the time; but it was testing my patience, and my anxiety and fear were increasing. I was frustrated, bordering on misplaced anger, definitely scared and close to despair. It seemed that the gods were conspiring against my best efforts to get help for my son.

One day, I was talking with an acquaintance, a doctor that worked at the local Nooksack Indian Tribal Health Clinic, Mary Ellen Shields. As I was sharing my experience with the autism clinic, she looked at me and said, *"I am friends with the medical director, Chuck Cowan. Let me give him a call."* Give him a call? How 'bout a bat signal with fireworks, flares and a happy dance! I was thrilled! And true to her word she did exactly that. Two days later I got a call from Dr. Cowan and Ry was fast tracked. We had an intake set for the next month.

The time period from Ray Soriano's comments and the intake appointment at UW spanned about five to six months, but truthfully, it's hard to recall exactly. Life was a blur, I was scrambling to keep my head above water and there are periods from this time that are lost to me forever.

However, my strongest and most enduring memory from that time was Ry's laughter or lack thereof.

As I said before, he was an effervescent, bubbly toddler. This child awakened most mornings and from naps happily chatting to himself and giggling - that sweet, mischievous laughter that only a small child can emit, melting hearts with it's unbridled joy. When Ry began to regress, the laughter disappeared from our home. It was a sadness I could not reconcile. It was devastating. There was nothing I could do to bridge the gap of my world and the place where he was trapped. Interminable days stretched into weeks and months and I was beginning to fear that I had forever lost my son to his autism, a world I could not breach. Shortly before taking him to Seattle, I walked in the door from work and heard giggling! My son, the child I thought I had lost WAS BACK, though not the same. He was Ryan 2.0 and I had to recreate what I knew about him and relearn how to meet his needs, I became Mom 2.0.

So, I gathered up my beautiful boy and headed south to the big city, hopeful. The University of Washington Autism Clinic is not directly attached to the campus, it is kind of down the hill, close to Seattle Children's Hospital.

Its stand-alone building is not remarkable of its own accord, but for me it was the Holy Grail. I was finally going to get answers and be rescued from what was reinventing Ryan. After filling out a gazillion forms and questionnaires, all while trying to herd Ry, we were led into an examination room. Dr. Cowan walked in and got to work. He looked Ry over, talked with him, asked me lots of questions, reviewed my paperwork and gave me a preliminary summary.

He was fairly certain that Ry was high functioning autistic but blood work was in order to rule out Fragile X. Ry demonstrated echolalia, hyperlexia, stereotypies and tics. I sat there for a minute, on information overload, and I knew I was out of my league and I needed coaching.

Fragile X: Genetic disorder on the X chromosome, affecting males more than females, displays as moderate to severe intellectual disability, long narrow face, big ears, hyper mobile joints and (10% have) seizures. Thankfully, Ry tested negative! Small victory!

Echolalia: The non-sensical repeating of another person's words throughout conversation. What that means is that if I asked Ry *"Do you want dinner?"*, he would reply, *"Do you want dinner?"* To compound his speech anomalies, when Ry came back as version 2.0, he had his pronouns flipped. He called himself "you" and everyone else "I". I get his point. Like before, if I said *"Ry, do you want dinner?",* he identified himself as you and would reply, *"You want dinner"*, not *"I want dinner".* It's quite brilliant actually, but it's not how we are supposed to sort out language and I became a full-time interpreter teasing out my child's Yoda-speak for everyone.

Hyperlexia: Compulsion to read exhibited by small children. It is hard to describe how crippling hyperlexia can be with a child like my son, but perhaps I can put it into context. At my local mall, the distance from the side door to Baby Gap is approximately 75 yards or eight storefronts. One day I needed to go to Baby Gap to get clothing for Ry. It took us over an hour to cover the distance from front door to store. He had to stop at every sign and read every word, sometimes twice. If I tried to hustle him, his body would begin to vibrate, becoming rigid... nervous system pushing back at my best attempt to intervene. This was not an isolated experience but our day -to -day rhythm navigating the written language.

Stereotypies: Repetitive motor movements such as rocking and hand flapping. Ry had a bank of these behaviors that are hard to describe. He would place his open hand just to the side of his eye and while closing it into a tear drop, drawing it laterally towards his ear just to the outer margin of his peripheral vision. Another favorite was to place his hand, loose fist forward, on his forehead, flexing and extending his index finger. One day I decided to give it a go. It was remarkably soothing. It seems to me that Ryan's nervous system was overwhelmed and he was creatively finding ways to soothe himself.

Tics: Self-stimulating behaviors and the one aspect of Ry's autism that really pushed/pushes my patience. Ryan's tics have ranged from throat clearing (every five to ten seconds) to ear twisting to nose mashing. These behaviors actually hurt and he readily admits that, but he continues to do them when he is stressed. I think they distract him from the external world that he struggles against, but it makes me a little crazy to see his self-injurious behavior. We continue to play tug of war as I remind him to keep his hands from his face. For the record, Ry is crushing me with his dogged perseverance.

And so, I left U.W. armed with a new vocabulary and officially entered the world of parenting a special needs child. Next up... Acceptance.

Acceptance

It never occurred to me that I could "cure" Ryan of his autism. I did not believe, like so many other desperate parents looking for causality, that vaccines or the environment were to blame or that chelation would rid him of heavy metals that may be causing his condition. But, I held firmly to the belief that I could somehow, some way, change the outcome of his life. After the shock and sadness of his diagnosis, it took me days, weeks, to come to that conclusion and I was hell-bent on making sure that this little boy, my trusty sidekick, was going to have his fullest and most productive life possible.

I believed that Ryan's autism was inherited, plain and simple. It seemed a conflux and combination of genetic material from both his paternal and maternal heritage. By all accounts, his paternal grandfather, Wes, was obsessive/compulsive and displayed Asperger's traits. These characteristics served him well as a bank Vice-President, but not so much for his twin children and my son. Lee, Ryan's father, also had OCD, Asperger's characteristics and readily raged at inanimate objects. The positive aspects - he was an exceptional athlete, national championships and Olympic team qualifier, very bright, his

Ph.D. earned in 5 academic quarters and was musically gifted. The downside? Dishes had to be washed clockwise, shirts folded with the left side facing upward, tools hung on the wall of the shop, neatly fitting into the outline drawn for them (they could not be placed in any other fashion without repercussions) and an irrational fear that someone would think he wasn't smart. I could go on and on, but I think the reader can see how he needed to control his environment in order to "function" and reduce stress... and it impacted his happiness.

On the other side of the genetic aisle was my family. My mother has her own wonderful set of "quirky" characteristics that most would never notice. Besides being remarkably, almost freakishly, intuitive and empathic, as a child she had an "imaginary" friend and they would chat for hours in a world no one else was invited to join or perhaps a space where she was reconciling her difficult surroundings. There are other stories about complex, patterned finger tapping, ability to visualize 3-D molecular compounds, and a lifetime of uncanny déjà vu moments. But the mother I know struggles with contextualizing things and can get overwhelmed with prolonged social activity and noise. It's not to say she withdraws, she just needs to decompress after a bout of raucous interactions and seeks a quiet place to settle her nervous system. And for the record, she is the funniest storyteller I have ever known. Our formal family dinners usually ending with one or all of us in tears when she was/is on a roll! What did Ry inherit from her? He received an incredible and innate empathy, heart sense and a linguistic capacity that leaves me in awe.

I also have my own set of secret traits. As a child I would spend hours on the back patio watching ants track across the cement, their complex trails intriguing me to no end. Then there is the counting. For example, as I fill my coffee pot each morning (six cups), I silently and sometimes unknowingly count to six and that is the exact amount of time to fill the pot to six cups. I never practiced that, it is just one of those quirky things I do and only recognized the consistency of it in the last year or so. Tile floors in bathrooms are the worst! I find myself counting the tiles on the x and y-axis to get the total tiles on the floor -- go figure. I also look for and find patterns in objects with ease. Give me a suspended ceiling in a doctor's office and I am entertained, finding patterns in the pinpricks of texture in each tile. These mental exercises don't seem to exhaust or calm me and perhaps I feel compelled to do them, but I think I have always been this way. This is how I'm put together and I had no idea other people didn't also do it until recently. So, what did Ryan inherit from me? My choice in life partners, mitochondrial DNA, a stubborn streak a mile long (okay, two miles), and I would like to believe a glass-half-full attitude towards life. He never got the hang of ants!

Finding causality for autism is a treacherous landscape. It seems each day there is a new announcement on Autism Speaks or similar resource sites that suggests that there may be a genetic component, or that maternal diet and illness during pregnancy can contribute, or paternal age at fertilization is a major influence. As a biologist I would agree that causality is as complex as the disorder itself and that each autistic child has a myriad of genetic and environmental impacts that may shape the destiny of their disorder.

So, in the spring of 2003, I had diagnosis in hand and no idea what future he would have. It certainly was not the one I had imagined for him the first time I felt him move while pregnant. What I did know was that acceptance did not mean surrender, quite to the contrary. Now I knew the name of the enemy that was ravaging my son and was prepared to learn every nuance of this disorder to insure that Ry could meet his full potential. I laugh now thinking about my naïveté. Learn every nuance of autism? Every time I was bold enough to think I had Ryan figured out, he proved me dead wrong. After a couple of years of this, I began referring to it as a touch and go. Whenever I thought he was coming in for a landing, nose up, gear down, headed for the runway, course predictable, the wheels would touch the tarmac for an instant and **boom!** He was taking off in a different, unexpected direction, jets blasting ninety to nothing and I was left there, shaking my head. And I never saw it coming. After 17 years of being his mother, the learning curve has not gotten any less steep.

Public School: Part I

Most health professionals agree that early intervention is paramount to helping autistic children deal with their social and learning deficits. As mentioned before, at the time of Ry's diagnosis, we lived in a one-horse town. The school district in the area consisted of two elementary schools, a combination junior/senior high and a special program that would become my lifeline for a year. Attached to the district office was the Center for Families and Children. The director, Vicky Hubner, had previously worked at my college in the job that Ray Soriano occupied. Vicki was a gifted early childhood educator and the Nooksack Valley School district gave her carte blanche to create a developmental pre-school for autistic children. Here I was, living in the middle of nowhere, or at least next door to it, and there was an award winning child development center less than three miles from home. Will wonders never cease? Blessings everywhere!

In no time flat, I had Ryan registered for the 2003 school year and we were on our way. Vicki coached me through the special education process. Not only did I have a special needs son, I now had a special education student. First order of business was creating an Individualized Education

Plan (IEP) to meet Ryan's needs. For me, the IEP represented (represents) a contract made between the school district, school, parent(s) and student with regard to providing clearly delineated educational goals, therapies, supports and best practices. At that first meeting, his IEP was a new educational landscape that I was trying to understand with limited success. Ry's IEP covered far ranging items found under the annual goals header. He was going to be helped with social/emotional, adaptive, fine/gross motor, cognitive and oral language development. Really? Is that all? As each area was explained to me, three thoughts went through my mind:

> 1. *Thank you, thank you, thank you for helping my son*
> 2. *I think I am getting the hang of this*
> 3. *How on earth are y'all going to accomplish this monumental laundry list of interventions?*

I was overwhelmed, curious and hopeful.

As we finished up our meeting, Vicki handed me a booklet, *Notice of Special Education Procedural Safeguards for Students and Their Families* and explained to me that Ryan, Lee and I had legal rights. Legal rights! I wasn't entirely sure what that meant, but I took the booklet, thanked her and headed home.

That evening I read the information from cover to cover, twice. I couldn't undo Ryan's condition, but I could be a dogged advocate with the backing of the federal and Washington State governments! With the law in my corner, I packed Ry off to school every weekday, hopeful that our world was going to be okay.

There are two take-away messages in the preceding paragraphs:

First, early intervention is key to maximizing positive gains for autistic children. If you suspect that your child, grandchild, family friend's child, or student displays any autistic-like characteristics, do not hesitate, pick up the phone and make an appointment now, have that awkward conversation with your friend - whatever it takes, get the child assessed. I am quite certain that Ryan's pediatrician was close to suggesting that Ry get help, she intimated concerns for a year, but Ray Soriano beat her to the punch. Because he saw Ry on a daily basis, Ray had a clearer picture of my son's behavioral and social limitations. He bravely took that first step, had that very uncomfortable conversation with me, and Ry got the help he needed earlier.

Second, you have rights and with that, a voice. Parents and guardians, you have the law on your side, no one can take that away and it is empowering. Public schools have to provide the support outlined in an IEP and if you suspect or know that they aren't, you have options at the district and state level. Do not be afraid to ask questions and challenge. The squeaky wheel gets the grease! And if you are not a native speaker, request an interpreter so that you can fully understand the process and have the confidence to communicate your concerns. I cannot tell you how many times I challenged my local school district to get continued classroom support for my son. At times it was an exhausting and daunting task, but worth every argument I had to endure on Ryan's behalf. It entailed letters, e-mails, phone calls and trips to the district office. More than once I was on the phone with the State Superintendent's office or filing a citizens complaint against a district employee because they refused to honor my child's I.E.P.

So, back to the story...

There are so many transformative moments that come across our life path - you can call them fate, destiny or plain dumb luck. But whatever label you use, the key is to recognize them for their significance. Meeting with Vicki Hubner was one such moment. She taught me how to advocate for my son and gave me a focused voice that would serve me well as I traversed the public school system. This was a high stakes game and she mentored and guided me through the process so that I could tackle problems with strength and conviction.

For those that have known me for any length of time, you have heard me say more than once that Ryan has angels. No, not the little chubby, cherubic, celestial critters with wings, but people that showed up in our lives at the most opportune time. When I was lost and at my wit's end, these angels were there to listen, guide, support, advocate and take some of the weight off of my shoulders. So far you have met three of them: Mary Ellen Shields, Ray Soriano and Vicki Hubner, and if you have the patience, I will continue to introduce them along the way. What Ryan's journey would look like without them, who can say, but I am so thankful that our paths intersected in the most unexpected way and that they offered, with an open heart, to help my Ryan. Many thanks to those three people, they are forever members of this family's village.

This section is written by Ryan Cunningham:

I believe the I.E.P. helps to counsel me as I continue through school. They (I.E.P.) help me to become a better student by providing me information about goals. Having people talk about my disability at an I.E.P. feels okay to me because it is a part of who I am.

And Then There Was Music

As soon as Ryan could walk he was playing the piano. At sixteen months he would toddle over to the old upright piano and happily plunk along while Lee was playing a song. As time progressed, his talent became apparent. Within a few years he was playing moderately complex songs by ear with an ease that was surprising.

There are so many stories to tell about how music has transformed his life. For us, the piano was the only real vehicle that gave me any insight into his emotional spaces.

When he was about seven, after a particularly bad day at school, Ry came home and went straight to the piano. At this age, he was still struggling with verbal communication, emotional expression and was beginning to have increasingly intense and frequent tantrums/meltdowns. The classroom was a very stressful environment and Ry lashed out at stimuli he was unable to filter - nervous system overload. I was grasping at straws trying to find any vehicle of communication that would allow me a glimpse of what it was like to live in his skin. As I listened to him play one afternoon, for reasons I can't recall, I asked him to play his day. He stopped, staring at the keys, perhaps considering my request, and began to play a cacophony of disjointed sounds that were difficult to hear. I stood there dumbstruck and sadness coursed through my being. I had hit pay dirt, had finally found a meaningful way for him to communicate with me, but my heart wasn't prepared for the results.

From that point forward, I asked Ryan to play his day, a person, an argument, and emotions more than a few times - actually, quite a lot. He astonished me with the emotional depth and accuracy of his musical renditions of his world. My favorite play back was just after he and I had a disagreement. Once we both settled, feeling reasonable, I asked him to play me. My small child began to bang and bang on the piano in minor keys. Think an angry version of *The Phantom of the Opera* and you get the gist. I couldn't really disagree with his assessment. I suppose that is exactly what I sounded like and I had to own up to it. From that point forward, I tried, often failing, to temper my tone while talking to him and was judicious about asking him to give me emotional musical feedback.

As I said earlier, Ry played the piano by ear. He never had formal training and I was not going to push the issue. The last thing I wanted to do was push him into lessons so that he learned to hate the piano. One morning as I walking through the sitting room en route to the kitchen, Ry had one of my old music books on the piano and was playing a song. You know those moments as a parent when you look over to your small child and they are reading a book or newspaper upside down? This situation was reminiscent. Ry had the music book opened to a song, but that was not what he was playing - he was faking it. I stopped and told him if he was going to use a songbook, he needed to learn to read music, thought nothing of my statement and continued my path to the coffee pot. That was Saturday. The rest of the weekend Ryan sat at the piano playing music while consulting his laptop.

Monday after school, he had the book out again and was playing, but something was different. He was playing the song! Curious, I turned the page and said, *"Play this song"*. And he played it! I turned pages again. "*How about this song?*" He performed flawlessly! In a period of forty-eight hours my child had taught himself to sight read music! From that point forward he spent an inordinate amount of time researching and teaching himself complex music theory, decoding the universal language. I began to get a peek at his gifts for decoding - reading by three, music by six or seven, computer and foreign languages soon to follow.

As time went on, people began to recognize Ryan's talent. There were instances of him sneaking into the elementary school auditorium because the piano was stored there - he just needed to play, time to decompress. I received more than a few phone calls from the front office reporting an outburst because he wasn't allowed access. The maintenance man on campus, Scott, would shake his head and say, *"Why don't they let him play? It's stupid."* I couldn't have agreed with him more. Over time the schools began to recognize that letting him play was a good strategy to calm his nerves when he felt overwhelmed. Scott, you are a genius.

Music was also a pathway for peer acceptance. Ryan had a gift and the kids recognized and appreciated it. The small kid that would stand alone and apart on the playground banging on a metal pipe with his ear against the pole was finally being approached by other children and it felt like maybe things were going to be okay. Eventually. He had his first public performances at his seventh and eighth grade end-of-school-year talent shows and brought the house down both times. Students went wild, came out of their seats and gave him a standing ovation! My son found a way to connect to his peers and it served him well as he headed into high school. He was the kid that was an "amazing" piano player and was no longer pigeon-holed into that odd kid space. He had an avenue for connection and a heap of truly kind kids that rallied around him.

I don't know that I ever understood the extent of Ry's musical talents until he got into high school. The summer before his ninth grade year, as was our practice, we toured his new school before any other students were on campus. This strategy helped Ry get his bearings without having to navigate the unpredictability of other people. It kept him from shutting down and helped him transition more easily. As we were walking through the halls with his special education teacher, Mary, we passed an open classroom and this guy sticks his head out the door and says, *"Do you sing?"* Ryan began to twist his ear, stressed, and said. *"I think so."* So, off to the counseling office and Ry was signed up for Men's Choir. We entered the world of Andy Marshall and the Squalicum High School chorale.

Choir was a gift to this family. Ry was learning to collaborate and perform with a group of peers. He was forced to receive constructive criticism and to act accordingly to Andy's tough classroom behavior standards. The choir kids were sweet, kind, supportive and helped herd Ryan through the social demands of this group.

Part way into Ry's first year, Andy pulled me aside and asked if I knew that Ry had perfect pitch. Nope, I hadn't a clue! In truth, I didn't even know what that meant. Andy had been suspicious and tested him. Basically, hum a note, play a key on the piano, play a few bars and Ry could tell you the note or what key the music was in instantly. He could decipher/decode the vibrations. Pretty cool! The obvious advantage, Ry could tell Andy exactly which singer in the choir was off key. The disadvantage, I had to tune our piano.

Andy also firmly believed Ry could find independence through musical performances. That perhaps he could play accompaniment for churches or choirs. In an attempt to draw out those skills, Andy had Ry accompany the school choir on numerous occasions. It gave Ry much needed performance practice, exposure to the public and confidence. In addition, he referred us to a music professor at the local university.

Ry had an uncanny skill for writing musical scores. It was never an original piece, but he would listen to some music, write the score and then create an adaptation or new arrangement. He began doing this around age twelve and it was becoming very commonplace and by the age of fourteen, the house was littered with his creations and manuscript paper. I decided to get Ry's abilities tested. I wanted to understand the depth of his musical gifts. I was never an accomplished musician and was unsure about Ry's abilities in relation to the "norm". A music professor from the local university tested Ry for perfect pitch, and musical memory, both of which Ry excelled at, and then he did something I had never seen. He asked Ry to play a simple song in the key of C. Ry sat there for a moment and began to play. Then he was asked to play it in F sharp. Okay, he waited about fifteen to twenty seconds and he did it. How about A minor? Fifteen to twenty seconds later, and the song was transposed. And that was how I learned that Ryan had musical savant gifts! But what to do with those talents? The teacher threw out words like Julliard and focused hard work, but I knew that wasn't Ry's path - at least not yet. This story will not end for some time and it is up to him to find his path. All I can do is support and guide him and provide opportunities so that he can refine his gifts if that interests him.

Most autistic children are gifted or very pre-occupied by a particular subject or activity. Their depth of focus and understanding of their special interests can be mind blowing. I dream of a day when the school systems can tap into these special gifts to foster skill sets that better suit the child's ability for employment as they transition into adulthood. I also realize that our current education funding does not prioritize this student subset and that leaves educators very little in the way of resources to help this special population.

[The portion below was written by Ryan Cunningham.]
Ryan has also worked with the judges of several San Juan Music Educators' Association Solo & Ensemble contests, to present for them several distinct pieces (including J. S. Bach's Prelude No. 1 from The Well-Tempered Clavier), and currently sings in the Squalicum High School Concert Choir, conducted by Jason Parker (the previous conductor, Andrew Marshall, has since left Squalicum for the International School of Bangkok). Messrs Parker and Marshall helped me find opportunities in adulthood, as I love to play the piano and sing.
To Ryan, music means a lot: music can convey emotions that words alone can't convey. Musical pieces do not have to have lyrics to convey such deep emotions as strong happiness or crying sadness, and those

lyrics (which are, by definition, poetry) also do not have to have music accompanying them to convey those same emotions.

[The portion written by Ryan Cunningham finishes here.]

Widowed

By March of 2004, Lee had been receiving medical treatment for twenty-two months. It's odd how easily one changes gears from the normalcy of day -to- day life to caretaking and helping someone exceed prognosis. When Lee was diagnosed with cancer, the doctor gave him three to six months to live. I promptly fired the physician that put limits on Lee's life expectancy, headed south for treatment and began the process of becoming well versed in large cell carcinoma of the lung... right lung to be specific.

During the duration of Lee's cancer, he endured 2 surgeries, weeks of radiation, five rounds of heavy duty chemo, walking pneumonia, pneumococcal pneumonia, thrush and staph infection. Not to mention the chemo-brain that seemed to slowly impair his gray matter and amplify an already unpredictably volatile personality.

The treatments that were prolonging his life were crushing his immune system - specifically the functioning of the bone marrow. His white blood cell count steadily declined, then plummeted and that put him at high risk for secondary infections. In addition, his red blood cell count was also deteriorating and, therefore he spent the better part of twelve months drifting from slight to severe anemia. It was a tough and exhausting road and Lee was wearing thin. And in truth, so was I. I was trying to manage Lee's illness, get Ry much needed therapies, run a household and hold down a job. It was a busy time.

On March fifteenth, at the dinner table, Lee turned to me, pointing to his chest and said his lung felt weird. His *left* lung specifically. He had just finished a potent round of antibiotics for a staph infection and his last MRI showed the tumor in the right lung shrinking - a small victory. However, I never ignored the slightest hiccup. I told Lee that I wanted him to make an appointment and get to the doctor's office immediately. He wanted to give it a day or two before calling and I knew arguing with him was fruitless. At this point in the process, Lee was becoming more combative about his care. He was tired of meds, needles and being out of control. I have no idea if he ever made that appointment - he never shared and I am not sure I asked, me being exhausted from trying to keep up.

On a Wednesday, I came home from work and Lee was sitting on the great room floor, half dressed and looking at me, confused. As he tried to speak, his words made no sense - gibberish. I knew this was not good. He was hypoxic, low blood oxygen, and his brain was struggling to make sense of his environment. To compound the situation, Ry's school bus was due to arrive at any moment and I was desperate to simultaneously protect Ryan and get Lee to the hospital. Ambulance service in our area was sketchy at best, so I called his sister and brother-in-law and they transported him to the Emergency Department, stat.

Torn between having Ry at the E.R. for hours or at home quiet, I chose to stay put with my four year old son, impatiently and anxiously waiting for a call from the ER doctor. The report - the mass in Lee's left lung was the size of an orange and that Lee's situation was dire. I stopped, thought, and said, *"The right lung, the tumor is in the right lung"*, and that's when I knew that Lee was dying. He had contracted viral pneumonia and within forty-eight hours it had taken over his good lung.

What does a person do? I had a young autistic child that was barely verbal, traumatized by his father's illness, confused by transitions and my family lived on the east coast. I had some support, but not enough to feel comfortable leaving my son overnight with someone and my husband was dying. I stayed with Ry, knowing I could do nothing for Lee and hoping that he would survive the night. He did.

When I got to his hospital room early the next day, the scene was surreal. Lee was hooked up to an oxygen mask and a volunteer was holding it off of his cheeks. The mask was ill fitting and Lee kept trying to remove it. His nail beds were tinged blue and he was floating in and out of consciousness, mumbling incoherently, seemingly arguing with himself. I felt that he was working out his death. It was a scene I was unprepared for, but after a moment I got my bearings and oriented myself to the situation.

Lee never wanted to die in the hospital and had shared that with me more than once. His father had contracted lung cancer that metastasized to the brain (an uncanny family legacy) and he died in the hospital. I had promised Lee I would do everything I could to prevent that from happening to him. So, here I was, at the hospital stuck with hard decisions. I wanted Lee to die at home and honor his wishes, but I didn't want Ryan exposed to that process. I was afraid of long reaching trauma and Ry was already suffering emotionally because of his father's illness. Once I saw Lee in the hospital, I realized that he was going to die there. He could not be safely transported back to the house and these thoughts were confirmed by Hospice. I requested comfort measures, stayed by his side and helped him die. He passed away that Friday evening. One workweek was all it took to go from a comment at the dinner table to death and I was reminded of the tenuous nature of our existence and how quickly life can go south.

According to Lee's wishes, there was not going to be a funeral, memorial or burial. As odd as that felt, it was what he wanted. I had him cremated and let his adult children spread his ashes. Ryan and I did not participate and I always questioned that decision. Lee's oldest child had issues with me and I felt that it was important for them to say good-bye to their father without my being there. I had been grieving Lee's death for twenty-two months and I was there when he passed - spreading his ashes was not part of my closure. But maybe it should have been part of Ryan's process. It's hard to know for sure. When I told him his daddy had gone to heaven, there were no tears, questions, or tantrums, nothing to indicate that Ry was hurting or confused. I didn't assume that he was okay, I kept a very watchful eye on him, but I had little indication that he was aware of this loss. If someone tells you that an autistic child doesn't know what is going on, they are wrong! Ry knew his world had changed, but he couldn't articulate that verbally or non-verbally and I couldn't see it - there were no tell-tale signs. I firmly believe that is how he got emotionally stuck in his little kid space for so many years. His world had come crashing down around him and he had no voice.

I tried to stay in the home that Lee and I built. It was a beautiful space, familiar to Ry and I had supportive and caring neighbors. Ry was attending a developmental kindergarten for autistic children at the local elementary school and was getting the help he needed. But I soon realized that I had to move to town. I was having difficulty maintaining my home and property, finding after school care for Ryan and my job was a solid thirty-minute drive one way. I needed to simplify and compress my world so that Ry and I could move into the next phase of our lives. Eight months later I closed the door on that life and began to create new spaces for Ry and me.

I didn't really know how I was going to raise my son by myself. It was daunting surviving the day-to-day rhythm of our lives together. I was pulled in many directions. I was desperate to keep my professional life separate from personal. I had piecemealed a full time position at the local community college, but not the security of tenure. I was becoming more and more concerned about Ry's behaviors in school and the ability to find after school care that would deal with his limitations. At the time I had no idea that things would get much, much worse before we landed on our feet and could breathe freely - sort of.

[The following segment was written by Ryan Cunningham.]
A then-new world - a world without Ryan's father Lee - would then have been difficult to be seen through Ryan's eyes. Lee's death was out of Ryan's control (he died of pneumonia due to lung cancer from too much smoking).
But the life that Ryan now lives in is incredible - although still a work in progress. Almost every day, he feels amazing, respectful, and empathetic.
[The segment written by Ryan Cunningham ends here.]

Public School Part II

Moving into our new home meant registering with the local school district. I worked very hard to insure that Ry was entering his new school after the winter break. It gave us the needed time and opportunity to get accustomed to our new home without having to navigate a new school simultaneously.

The school district really didn't know what to do with my son. We were armed with an IEP, but they didn't have the resources to provide an instructional aide for him in the middle of the school year so that he could be mainstreamed into a kindergarten classroom. There was no such thing as a developmental pre-school or kindergarten at that time and the only remaining option was the life skills classroom on the other side of town. Everyone quickly agreed that this was not a good fit. His developmental disability was much less severe than his peers and his ability to read and write put him light years ahead of this group of children. After six weeks of frustration, I was finally able to get him moved into a different classroom and was hopeful that things were going to work out. In the end, we limped through the school year with Ry not getting the support he needed and me doubting my decision to move.

First grade did not start smoothly either. I decided to take a chance on a local private school that convinced me that they could provide Ry with the educational support he needed to be successful. The teacher to student ratio was extremely attractive and he was enrolled. That lasted about five days. The head mistress had never followed up with Ry's previous teachers, as I had requested, and therefore hadn't a clue about the extent of support he required. I was upset, frantic and astounded by the lack of due diligence or best practices and pulled a confused Ry (he never forgot that experience) from that school and registered him at our local neighborhood public school.

Ry's new classroom was a busy space with lots of children and stimuli. By this age, when Ry was introduced into a new environment, he needed to frantically explore every single space, nook and cranny, over and over again, day after day. His compulsivity and impulsiveness were a problem and could be crippling to him and the teacher. His behavior was time consuming, disruptive and exhausting. He had difficulty transitioning from one activity to another and if he was redirected, he would meltdown in ways that were impressive: screaming, crying and charging the teacher, fighting against the ability to deal with new stimuli.

His first grade teacher, Lisa McAlpine, knew Ryan needed help quickly and got to work strongly advocating for him. She requested an instructional aide and began communicating with me regularly in order to better understand my son's needs. She was my newest lifeline and I was holding tightly to her positive energy, master teaching, empathy and desire to give Ry a chance.

The school district did not have a readily available aide, all of them had been assigned to other students, as we were late to the game having tried the private school route first. So they called a gentleman that was a retired teacher and asked if he would be willing to work part-time with Ry. I am not certain what transpired, but he met with Ry and Lisa and decided to leave retirement and go back to work part-time. I later discovered that Rick had been a special education teacher with expertise in and empathy for autism spectrum disorders. I was relieved and grateful that my special boy was going to get much needed and mandated extra support and thrilled that his aide was male! No gender bias, but I knew Ry needed positive male role models after losing his father and Rick helped to fill part of that void.

So with a feisty, wicked smart and proactive teacher and an extraordinary gifted aide, Ry began to make progress. It might be noted that progress at that time might have been defined and measured by the number and intensity of tantrums he would have in class, if he interacted with his classmates or stayed seated for any length of time. It was a trying time for Ryan's nervous system, but there was a team of educators committed to helping him.

One of my favorite memories from this year was the creation of *Ryan's Quotes, First Edition*. Ry had a funny way of communicating and some of the things he would say were flat out funny, precocious and endearing. At the end of the school year, I was presented with a couple of typewritten pages of *Ryan's Quotes* compiled by Lisa and Rick. We sat in the classroom at the end of the year and read them. They were pearls from my Yoda-speak kiddo. It felt good to be tickled by my child's world perspective and I felt the caring and love that both of these people shared for Ry. From that point forward, each year until Ry left middle school and Rick finally retired, Rick, and then later, his other aide Ellyn, would present end-of-year *Ryan's Quotes* to me.

As Ry proceeded through grade school, he continued to get support to improve his social interactions, occupational and physical therapies and speech language. I can distinctly remember meeting with the school psychologist in Ry's second year when she showed me a collection of headshots with different facial expressions. The special education team was trying to help Ry navigate nuanced, non-verbal behavior cues in order to better understand the human condition and improve his connectedness. The psychologist explained to me that she was concerned because Ryan was not making any progress... as in zero percent. I sat there, listened and started to quietly laugh... of course he wasn't making progress. We, being his grandmother and me, knew that his mirror neurons (that collection of neurons that help us tease out facial expression, meaning and context) were foggy at best, but that wasn't the half of it. Ry did not see whole faces and never had. He would see someone's eyes, or see a nose and ear, but never the whole image of the face. He would slowly piece together bits of facial features but it would take him dozens of consistent encounters with someone before he would begin to slowly recognize them. If he saw me out of context, he would not recognize or acknowledge me until he heard my voice. Can you imagine how scary it was to have your child not recognize you? If we were in crowded public spaces, I had a death grip on his hand; fearful that he would get away from me and not be able to find me, or me him.

Another gift that Ryan began to master in second or third grade was the "what if" question. These questions were hypotheticals that typically answered themselves based upon his wording. I found them increasingly annoying and exhausting as he aged, plucking at my nerves. Dealing with 100+ of these a day was mind numbing. By this time, Ry had two aides, Rick and Ellyn. Ellyn was the master of deflecting the "what if question" without losing patience and with a sense of humor. She had superhero ninja powers and I tried to tap into them more than a few times. We still laugh at his questioning tenacity. At this point in Ry's education, Rick and Ellyn became the dynamic duo taking on autism one day at a time with grace, creativity, patience and love. And I'm still getting a daily battery of the "what ifs".

I don't know how to put Rick and Ellyn into a contextual framework with regards to their penultimate importance to me because of their dedication and care for my son. Rick provided the male role model that my child so desperately needed after his father died. He stalwartly guided Ryan from first to eighth grade. He took Ryan to Broadway musicals in which his son Bradley performed, thereby shaping Ry's musical love for Broadway. He accompanied Ry to a multiple day overnight field trip because he knew that I could not take those days from my job. He showed up for all of Ry's musical performances through graduation as well as a number of his athletic competitions. He showed Ryan love, caring and the consistency of being there for him. Ellyn was Ry's second Mom. She gently guided him through his academic day within behavioral boundaries and lots of patience. She survived his every manipulation with a smile on her face and an "*I don't think so*" from her mouth. She was with Ry part-time from second to fifth grade and would fill in oftentimes in middle school. Both of them were important to Ry's success and I had to fight tooth and nail every year to have them as a team. The school district was fearful that Ry would become dependent and attached to them. Umm, the fact that he is autistic, has a disability and very much needed consistency never occurred to the Director of Special Education, but that's another story for a later time, back to school.

At some point in his early years of elementary school, the idea of oppositional defiance disorder was batted around by the school's Special Ed. team. Ry increasingly struggled taking direction from adults, believing that he had the knowledge and ability to control his environment and act on his own best behalf and questioned if the adults around him had the skills to do their jobs correctly. In a word, he was argumentative. At first it seemed kind of quaint and cute. He was six when this started. But soon he began to challenge every adult that crossed his path and the behavior was not so precious anymore. Somewhere along the line, he began to fire individuals. He fired Rick, Lisa, Ellyn, the principal (Mary Anne Stuckart), the Special Ed. teachers and district staff - the list was becoming long and impressive. Of course, I was fired more times than I can recall and at age eleven Ry wanted to become emancipated. You cannot imagine his frustration when he discovered that you had to be fourteen and go before a judge!

So, what started as an entertaining behavior became increasingly disruptive at school and at home and both his teachers and I were exasperated. Ry's increased need to control his spaces began to steamroll by third grade. He was continually and frequently challenging his third grade teacher, Gay Fullner. Gay was a soft –spoken, dedicated teacher, exuding calm... and she was struggling to get a handle on Ry. He was insistent that she was not a capable educator and began to threaten her removal on a regular basis. As much as I tried, I could not rein him in.

One afternoon, coming home from work, I found a large cardboard box on the front porch -- a UPS delivery while I was away for the day. As I looked at the box, I realized it was from a publishing house. Odd!?! I had not ordered any books and most professional texts were delivered to my work place. Curious, I dragged the box into the house and immediately opened it; all the while Ryan, standing beside me, was becoming more and more animated. Inside the box was curricular materials used by the state of Washington for third grade teachers. Turning to Ry, I asked: "*Ry, did you purchase these books?*" He was thrilled and said, "*Yes!*" as he reached into the box. I stopped him and asked, "*Why*"? He told me he didn't think his teacher was doing her job and wanted to see what he was supposed to be learning. Seriously? My eight year old purchased curricular materials online; not video games, not toys. Shaking my head, a thought occurred to me - how? Asking Ry "how", I discovered that my REI credit card number had been memorized by him. Quick phone call, cancel the card and Ry and I had a long talk. The old card was placed in a picture frame and morphed into something I began to refer to as the frame of shame. It was hung in the hallway and served as a daily reminder of Ry's ability to out smart me. Over the next few years, the infamous frame of shame would acquire three more cards before Ry stopped his covert online purchasing behaviors.

(In particular, the original purchased work was part of a mathematics curriculum titled Investigations in Number, Data, and Space, being a later edition of the same curriculum then used by Sunnyland Elementary's teachers. The curriculum was published by Pearson Prentice Hall and previously by Dale Seymour Publications.) I know this doesn't require explanation, but the above description was authored by Ryan.

My takeaway from Ry's first five years of public education: pre-school through third grade:

- My sense of humor was inversely related to the number of tantrums Ry had or the number of phone calls I received from his school.
- Individuals make a difference for better or worse Some put up barriers while others are committed to illicit positive change. Hold your warriors close - they will advocate like crazy for your child and you - that can be the game changer you need to

survive the process. These were my angels and I was collecting them as fast as I knew how!

- A lawyer's business card presented at the district office or a phone call to the state superintendent's office is a really effective way to get a quick response to a problem in which you are being stonewalled.

- Knowing your rights as a parent is the strongest weapon you have to advocate for your child. You have the law on your side.

- Question everything and collect lots of information from other parents. There is no such thing as a dumb question and you can glean so much from others' experiences.

You Got This, Ry

My son Ryan was born with hypermobile joints, low muscle tone, gravitational insecurity, poor visual processing (depth perception) and impaired balance. He was delayed in sitting up, crawling and walking. As his skills improved over time and he began running, he could only go about ten to twenty feet before he would have to stop or fall down because his muscles and joints couldn't support his momentum. He was a proverbial house of cards.

His father and I were athletes and had always lived active lives. We enjoyed water and snow skiing, hiking, rock climbing and general all around out-of-doors mischief. Both of us were determined to give Ryan exposure to a variety of activities and provide him with the same active lifestyle that we enjoyed. By age two, it became apparent that it was going to take all of our knowledge and energy as physical educators, kinesiologists, and coaches with a large heaping spoonful of parental love to help Ry gain the skills and confidence in his physical abilities or lack thereof.

The Steeps:

Ryan never tried to climb out of his crib. Most parents are probably glaring at the page right now because their children repeatedly performed their Houdini feats on a daily basis. In my case, I had always thought, "*what a good baby*" and "*thank goodness*". It never occurred to me that Ry stayed put because it was too scary to give it a go. By age three, he could not climb up or down stairs solo and would come unglued on the playground if I suggested we play on the slide. My child was terrified of heights. That's not quite accurate. He was terrified of his inability to physically negotiate changes in upward and downward terrain. His struggles to find balance, coupled with a lack of depth perception, and muscles and joints that were sub-optimal performers, were the perfect combination to keep his feet firmly planted on the ground. In short, he had gravitational insecurity. The situation was so challenging, that when we moved into town, I would only entertain single story homes. Ry needed a house that felt safe and navigable to him and stairs were not in the cards. With that in mind, my dedicated realtor, Jeff, drove me to more than a few houses trying to find a situation that Ry and I could call home. It was a simple, small, one story ranch with an open floor plan. It was the perfect solve for his physical challenges, but we still needed to work out the rest of our environs.

I was patient and decided that hills and stairs were not that important in the grand scheme of things.... he was still small, I could still carry him and there were elevators at most public spaces - Hooray for the Americans with Disabilities Act. However, as Ryan aged, I had to become more and more creative in managing hills and stairs. One can only hip-carry a child for so long and I needed modifications. At four years of age, my little guy was becoming an even bigger guy and I needed to find other means to get him from point A to point B without destroying my posture.

The easy solution when we hiked was to put him on my shoulders. That tactic worked well for small stretches of trail, but if we had a long downhill section, my legs typically wore out before the trail leveled out. It was time consuming and exhausting, but worth it in every respect. Looking back on my photo album, I see picture after picture of us hiking and snowshoeing. Ry smiling and sitting upon my shoulders and me thrilled with our adventuring life. In time, he slowly began to experiment and challenge himself - getting better with each attempt and my shoulders thanked him.

In the end, Ryan's gravitational insecurity improved. He was able to navigate most inclines and descents, but frequently needed coaching and handholding initially. My child of limited ego still has no compunction saying, "*Mom, I need help*" as he is reaching his man sized hand toward me - trusting that I will be there, reaching back to help. As a side note, this past summer he conquered his fears and went up in a hot air balloon. Granted, the balloon only ascended to twenty feet above terra firma; but for Ry, that was an enormous success.

He still flatly refuses to go down escalators and I was abruptly reminded of that in the Atlanta airport this summer. As we approached a very short escalator on our way to baggage claim, I asked Ryan if he thought he could negotiate it. Looking at me, he decided yes, he would try. Grabbing his carry on luggage and his hand, we stood at the top of the escalator, I said, "*Ready?*" and he said, "*Yes*". As I stepped onto the first step, he balked and pulled away from my hand. I was going down and he was rooted above me. With luggage in hand, I began a superhero sprint up the escalator, falling, tearing a gash into my knee and bleeding everywhere: but thankfully reaching him. Ry twisting his ear said to me, "*I'm sorry. I don't think I was ready to try that yet!*" I looked at him, looked at my knee, and said, "*Yeah, I think that's true.*" He still consistently wants my help descending steep hills (hand holding here and there) and requires extra time when he runs cross-country. But considering all that he overcame, I think that's pretty darn good!

Time to Ride:

Like every other parent I know, I bought Ryan a tricycle when he was three. I thoroughly enjoyed cycling and was eager for him to learn. We were going to be a cycling family, or so I thought. Poor Ry could not coordinate his left and right leg to move asynchronously in order to power the pedals. He would be so excited to get on his little Radio Flyer, but within minutes he would erupt into tears from frustration because he couldn't power the bike. At this time, glider bikes were not part of the American cycling lexicon and I had never been to Europe, where they are found in abundance. I wasn't sure how to proceed and did not know that there were other options. I didn't want him to have negativity associated with bikes or any activity for that matter. Therefore, I begrudgingly put the trike away, only pulling it out intermittently to see if his coordination had improved enough. In the meantime, I purchased a bike trailer and would drag him all over God's creation - biking family achieved!

Once we moved into town, I decided that Ry could try a big boy bike with training wheels. He was older, his coordination was improving with physical and occupational therapy sessions, and I was hopeful. The bike was an epic fail. Ry still did not have the balance, coordination or depth perception to succeed. I didn't give up. But as he aged, it was becoming increasingly difficult to find training wheels that could support his weight. If he began to lose balance, the wheels would bend and fold, becoming useless. They were not designed for a seventy pound child. So, once again, I put away the bike for a bit, bought a tag-along bike and we were off again, sort of. It was challenging pulling him behind my bike. He was getting big enough so that the smallest inadvertent movement/tic from him would cause my bike to become unstable and swerve. But, we were still riding, just a bit slower.

Have you ever had one of those ah-ha moments? When you think, "*Of course! That will work? Why didn't I think of that before?*" The summer of Ry's ninth year, after walking around a local park and watching toddlers on glider bikes (finally making their U.S. debut), I decided to take the pedals and training wheels off of his bike. The goal was to push himself along, lift his feet, and glide for 1 second. Do it again, glide for 2 seconds, etc. By the time he hit a ten second glide, I was ready to put his pedals back on his bike and let him try riding again. I had created a glider bike for a fourth grader and was hopeful he would learn.

The morning of his tenth birthday, Ryan looked at me during breakfast and declared that he was ready to ride his bike!!! All right, you got this Ry! I reattached the pedals and we headed down our street to the trail, he got on his bike and took off. Just like that, Ry was a bike riding super hero! All he needed was an appropriate accommodation in order to succeed and I finally hit pay dirt. I never imagined the long-term significance of him mastering this skill until much later. You see, Ry will never drive, and learning to ride a bike was giving him skills for independence as he aged. Beside the fact that it gave us more adventuring possibilities and justified purchasing a tandem. Woohoo!

When asking Ry what learning to ride a bike has meant to him, he states, " *I think riding a bike is good exercise for me. It also gives me the independence I need to get myself to school and to appointments when I don't want to take the bus. "*

Water Wings:

Growing up in the South, learning to swim wasn't just for fun or a way to survive the summer heat, it was a necessity to keep children safe. Drowning was a reality shown on the evening news and parents had children in lessons by the time they could walk. I carried that attitude with me to the Pacific Northwest. Ry was going to learn to swim. I had no notions that he was going be a competitive swimmer, I just wanted him safe and competent around the water.

When he was four, I packed him up and we were off to swim lessons at the local athletic club. The instructors were super sweet, enthusiastic college kids and class size was small; however, there was too much stimuli and the noise level in the pool area was unbearable for Ry. Try as they might, the instructors could not get Ry to engage and more often than not, he disappeared into himself. He wasn't making progress.

One day, while at the pool, I ran into an ex-student of mine. She had been a returning adult in my anatomy and physiology sequence and was studying to become a physical therapy assistant. Julia had been giving swim lessons for years and was willing to teach Ry one-on-one, when other lessons were not occurring - a quiet space for Ry to learn. I leapt at her offer and we were off to the races. I really don't remember how many years she taught him and it's not important to the story. What I do know is that he learned to swim and that opened up a new realm of possibilities for us. Since learning to swim, Ry has surfed and snorkeled in Hawaii, swam in Panama, Barcelona and the Atlantic Ocean and paddles with me on our two person outrigger canoe (OC-2). More than once we have flipped that canoe, and every time we get back on it safely, I send Julia a little psychic thank you and blessing...

[The following section is written by Ryan Cunningham]
I love paddling the outrigger canoe. It makes me happy and it fills my heart with joy when I am on the water. I don't like flipping over in it, but I am getting better about not getting upset when it happens. My mom always makes sure I wear a Coast Guard approved personal floatation device.

Snow Time is Fun Time:
When Ry was eight and still not able balance on one foot, I decided it was time for us to try skiing. What was I

thinking? I must have blown a synapse. The bunny hill at the local ski area was a disastrous undertaking. Ry, between my knees with a death grip on a ski pole I had in front of him for support, and me hunched over, forearms under his armpits desperately trying to keep him upright. His hyper-flexibility, low muscle tone, newly acquired fear of speed, and gravitational insecurity continually caused his legs to collapse under him with us landing in a heap over and over again. I quickly determined, with Ryan's steadfast encouragement, that downhill skiing was not going to happen that day or anytime soon, maybe ever. Hmm, I began to conspire with myself... what about cross-country skiing?

We were in need of an adventure, so, what the heck, I packed our gear, grabbed my dear friend Nancy for support and we all headed to Manning, B.C. to give it a go. After a fair amount of "*I can't do this, Mom!*" and "*I am so done*", I got Ry to solo ski about ten feet This, after a solid thirty to forty-five minutes of him skiing between my knees with my arms wrapped around him to keep his little body upright. He was stoked, I was thrilled and a little bit subluxated, but happy for him/us. We were adding another activity to our checklist of fun. He couldn't go far or fast, but he could go.

These days, we take long weekends to the Methow Valley and I can barely stay ahead of him. He can manage gliding down most small hills, refining his skills and gaining confidence with each trip. There is still a bit of "*I can't do this!*". But Ry learned long ago that when I say, "*You are going to try until you fail*", that I will wait as long as it takes and that he is safe, and must try. He usually succeeds, surprising himself, but not me. One day, sooner than later, I won't be able to keep up with him unless I skate-ski and he will stop telling me what he can't do and continue showing me what he can accomplish.

It took years to get Ry a degree of athleticism. Creative accommodations, activity modifications and truckloads of patience, humor and love from me, family, friends, teachers, coaches and therapists helped Ry to land on his feet and be successful. He actively rides, hikes, runs and paddles. He is willing to take chances but remains very aware of his limitations and places distinct boundaries on himself and others. Long after he is done being my trusty sidekick, he will have the skills, desire and ability to take on new tasks with a sense of self-confidence and a basis for success. You got this Ry!

On the Edge

"*It feels like a tsunami, Mom!*" I sat there stunned, my heart shattering into tiny pieces. Here was my twelve year old son, finally articulating what it felt like when he slammed into one of his "tantrums" and I was speechless, listening to his pain. For him, they came on suddenly, without warning and consumed him, leaving him feeling self-defeated with regret; for everyone else, it was scary, shocking, confusing and uncomfortable. For me, it was day-to-day existence with my autistic son and I was frequently exhausted, at my wit's end, feeling isolated and frightened for my child's future.

I don't remember exactly when Ry's tantrums turned into something bigger than the little person's average meltdown. All of us have most likely witnessed the terrible two's, three's and four's, but I was continuing to deal with this as Ryan was completing his sophomore year in high school. I know the extreme and frequent episodes began sometime in the early years of elementary school, while he was still physically small and manageable. Perhaps it was third grade, but that is of no consequence. What is important is that one day, Ry's difficulty transitioning from one activity to another scaled from bothersome to volcanic and it consumed most of the emotional energy in our household.

I spent years trying to tease out the trigger(s) for his explosive, angry displays, trying desperately to avoid the emotional land minds, but couldn't nail down a consistent source. Transitioning between activities seemed to be the biggest problem and the most likely candidate. Asking him to shut down his computer so that we could run errands or go for a bike ride or getting him to stop playing piano in order to eat dinner were typical scenarios that I knew would ignite him. But other times, he would explode for reasons I could not ascertain, and I suspect he was in the same boat.

A typical outburst from Ry might begin with his body becoming rigid (coiled), standing on his tippy toes, arms rising above his head in a threatening manner, hands flapping, eyes going wide, face turning crimson, and him sweating. His voice would steadily increase in volume to the point of screaming and his ability to rationalize would vaporize. If he was really upset, he would begin sprinting through the house, banging into walls or throwing himself on the ground staying rooted there interminably, dead weight, then immediately springing up, running from room to room looking for things to crash or crash into. It was an intense display of fight or flight and the source of the threat was invisible to me. It happened ten to twenty or more times a day at its peak.

My immediate response was to try to re-direct him and, failing that, my goal was to keep him and me safe. I would typically capture him in mid-sprint and try to control him - yea, right! Control is a funny word. My definition of control might be different from most parents, but in the end, I think all parents can agree that preventing injury is paramount to the physicality of children becoming unglued and lashing out at hidden enemies consuming their safe place. Some days I was more successful than others, but I kept at it.

At first I tried the counting game. As he became inflamed, I would start counting, 1, 2, 3, 4, and if I got to 5, straight into timeout - Parenting 101. Well, "that worked", said no one ever! When your child is engulfed in an uncontrollable, visceral manner, no amount of counting or threats of timeout is going to change the behavior. Ry was on adrenalin overload, felt threatened and timeout made things worse and was meaningless. I needed a more effective strategy.

I distinctly recall being at a meeting at his elementary school and the special education expert turned to me and suggested a reward system to control Ry's behavior. "*Reward?*" My first thought, and yes, I held my tongue, was "*You go first and tell me how that works out!*" I struggled taking behavioral advice from someone that saw my child one hour a week, at best, in pull out special education sessions and I suppose I wasn't being very fair. But giving my child a treat to control his behaviors due to fixations and the sympathetic nervous system, was akin to giving an adult with PTSD a reward and believing things were going to improve with their condition. A weighted vest was also recommended. The conventional wisdom was that the vest would help him feel more grounded and less apt to standing up and charging around. I know that everyone was trying to help and be supportive, but they were living on the outside looking in and really didn't understand the day-to-day challenges that face parents of autistic children. I was desperate for tangible advice and was struggling with my child's increasing difficulties. Simply stated, there weren't any traditional strategies that improved or changed his behavior, but I soon learned how to calm him and redirect his energy when he was in full flight mode.

Ry and I were having a Saturday like any other Saturday, when all of a sudden he exploded because I wanted him to get off the computer (fixation) so that we could go to the Saturday Market. I had employed all of the transitioning tactics I knew. Thirty minutes before leaving I said, "*Ry, we are going to ride to the market, find a stopping place soon so that we can get dressed and head out the door.*" Ten minutes later, "*Hey Roo, I want us moving towards the door in twenty minutes.*" Ten minutes later, "*Ry, I need you to stop what you are doing so that we can go downtown*". BOOM! Ryan lost it and started the sprinting game through the house. On his second or third circuit, I was able to catch him and for whatever reason, I held him in a giant full-bodied bear hug, gently lowered him to the floor, softly laid on him and began to speak to him quietly, reassuring him that he was safe.

At first he resisted me, and man-oh-man, he was getting strong and I was tempted to let him go... but, for reasons unknown, I persisted, continuing the quiet mantra in his ear. In less than a minute, I could feel him slowly uncoil. His body was becoming less rigid, his breathing was slowing down and he wasn't fighting my efforts. Moments later (felt like a lifetime) he was relaxed, quiet and said he wanted to get his shoes on to go downtown. I crossed my fingers, let him go and he transitioned perfectly. I sat there and thought, "*What the hell just happened?*" It wasn't until much later, when I was learning about Temple Grandin's squeeze machine, that I realized that my application of equal pressure on Ry's body calmed his nervous system. It may seem like a small victory, but at that time it was a game changer and I secretly began to hope we could survive this stage.

Ryan's outbursts were not isolated to the household. He was also having increased difficulty in the classroom. In meeting after meeting, aides, teachers and administrators would ask me for suggestions to help quell Ryan's nervous system. I could offer anecdotal information, but Ry at home was not Ry in school and what worked for me wasn't going to work for them. But we kept strategizing trying to find a common denominator that would help. I believe the best tactic we employed was a common language. Everyone agreed that it was important for Ry to hear a consistent message from both home and school. All of us put our heads together to create a predictable, common communication framework. It seemed to help and was used throughout his high school years.

I recently asked one of Ry's elementary school aides (Ellyn) to describe a typical classroom meltdown:

"Ryan would be in his "happy place" drawing maps, seating charts, etc. When it was time to stop, he would *'HAVE TO FINISH!!'* He would swing his arms around to push me out of the way or cover his work so that no one could take it away or see it, sometimes dropping on the floor and crawling away talking in third person, no sense of personal space, so when walking, he might step on someone."

"In Ry's mind he was 'always right' "

"By 4th or 5th grade when he would have an outburst, we would leave the room and go for a walk, mostly around in circle outside, and he would argue his point, or ask what-ifs or fire all of us. The funny thing was that he never wandered off, he followed or walked beside."

Ry would also jump up from his desk and charge the teacher. This became an increasingly frequent problem as he aged. He had no intention to cause physical harm, he just needed to be seen, heard, "be right" and challenge authority. It was a behavior that stayed with him into high school. Can you imagine how frightening that would be from a teacher's perspective? I received more than a few phones calls from school.

Ry had a number of saving graces during this challenging period in his life:

1. He had a stubborn parent that did not pretend there was not a problem. I had the greatest respect and empathy for his teachers and his aides were my comrades in arms and I deferred to their expertise, time and time again. I also had a family and extended family that supported me, didn't judge me and had my back when I felt that I couldn't handle one more thing.

2. His teacher's were incredibly dedicated educators and they could see past Ry's difficulties and embrace the loving, caring child he was/is, my Buddha-boy. Every single teacher Ry had from first to twelfth grade bent over backwards to accommodate my son and had an important role in his success.

3. His instructional aides were my lifeline. These paraprofessionals worked their fannies off to give Ryan a fighting chance and they have become family. They were integral and central to Ryan's success. They guided his teachers and did the heavy lifting day after day. I am forever in their debt for their steadfast commitment to see

past Ry's disabilities and celebrate his awesomeness with compassion and a sprinkle of humor, here and there.

4. There were a number of special education teachers that really "got Ry" and advocated to the point of being at odds with supervisors. I loved their passion and advocacy for children that did not have a voice and for parents that were either exhausted beyond comprehension or had no idea what transpired in school on a daily basis.

5. And finally, the school administrators that supported me and made a conscious decision to advocate and support Ry and me instead of following the letter of the behavioral law and presenting obstacles instead of solutions.

[The next passage was written by Ryan Cunningham.]
Mr. Cunningham has changed very much since ninth grade, having developed a lot of additional behavioral skills and qualities (even though suffering in them after a subsequent concussion), and feeling better because there have been less behavioral issues in the school and much fewer at home and elsewhere.

I would like to leave the reader with a few final thoughts:

- Ry's behavioral difficulties are not the exception to the autistic rule. So many spectrum children struggle with over-stimulation, fixation and fear of their environment, and thus, they strike out.

- As a parent of a child that would frequently lose it at the grocery, home improvement store, or a friend's home, being judged as a bad parent because my child was acting out felt horrible and isolating. I think many people look at an older kid having a meltdown and assume that they are spoiled and the parents have lost control. I encourage and challenge people to stop, think and wonder if maybe, just maybe, that parent is struggling and on the brink of collapse just to get the grocery shopping completed and that their child struggles with hidden monsters no one can see. As a side note, I once overheard a manager at our local grocery store telling a customer that I was an amazing parent and Ry's outburst were because he was special. I love where I live.

- And finally, you can tell someone that they are an amazing parent. That's nice to hear, but more to the point recognize when they are grumpy, reactive or exhausted, it's not about them but their circumstances. Give them a wee bit of forgiveness and offer help, not judgment...

In His Own Words

Ryan has a way with words... *Ryanisms.* Whether it was or was not his intention, he inadvertently captured his perspective of the world in a fashion that was unique to him and his autism. I thought it might provide some insight if I included a chapter of *Ryan's Quotes*, short stories and poetry from his elementary school years and one poem as he has entered adulthood, his words and not mine, to describe how he was managing his world. Some of this is funny, some poignant, some insightful and maybe heartbreaking - it is up to the readers to decide for themselves. Enjoy!

Ryan's Quotes: First Edition (2005-2006):

- "I'm only six. I don't know how to answer that question."
- "Mrs. McAlpine, am I annoying you?"
- "I have only a 1% chance of finishing my job."
- "We're doing that today and today is tomorrow."
- While viewing a pantomime activity,"Sick, sick, I'm sick of it."
- "I will enhance this story with another song."

- When his pencil fell to the floor he screamed. I (Rick) responded, "It's all right." His response was: "It's all right, but it's not ok."
- "No, I make my mother do it."
- "How do you think Franny is feeling?" Ryan: "Pissed off!"

  (captured by Rick and Lisa)

Ryan's Quotes: Second Edition (2006-2007)

- "That's a positive denial."
- "Is this Ryan's bad joke week?"
- Ryan was asked to make a statement. He said something and then explained- "That's a scrambled statement."
- Ryan was asked to sit down Ryan: "I am not responding."
- "Ryan I am not going to argue with you." Ryan: "Then I'll argue with myself."
- Teacher: "Why did I ask you to do this?" Ryan: "For no reason."
- Mrs. G (teacher) asked Ry to ask her a question that he didn't know the answer to. There was a long silence. Ryan then quietly said, "I know more than you anyway."

- "I work catastrophically well!"
- "I have to ignore all adults!"
- At the end of a written reading response he has written: Major funding provided by Microsoft Home

  (captured by Rick and Ellyn)

A Terrible, Horrible, No Good, Very Bad Day
Short Story by Ryan Cunningham © 2008
(Based on *Alexander and the Terrible, Horrible, No Good, Very Bad Day*, [1972], by Judith Viorst, illus. by Ray Cruz)

First, I went on the bus but it took a different route through Sunset Square. That bothered me a lot. I was very upset! Next, I lost computer time because I would not log off. After that, I fell down on the playground and skinned my knee. Later, I never logged on with my password but only typed my username so the computer would not work. Then I had no music because the schedule changed. After that, I also had no lunch because I forgot my lunch bucket. Mom was still working at Whatcom Community College and forgot to pick me up at the YMCA! She was 30 seconds late. It was a terrible, horrible, no good, very bad day!!

Ryan's Quotes: Third Edition (2007-2008)

- "I think my mother should be here instead of me."

- Mr. A: "That's a good example Ryan." Ryan: "Think nothing of it. I am being polite."

- Choices were to read or write. Ryan: "But my brain tells me to draw."

- Throwing a fit in the library. Mr. A: "Please stand up." Ryan: "I can't. I'm glued to the floor."

- "I have to memorize what you tell me, so I know why."

- Reading question: What would have been the worst part of the adventure? Indians, camping, animals? Ryan: "I'm going to a motel."

- Ryan, what are you doing? Ryan: "I am doing what you are doing."

- "I was demonstrating what not to do."

- Reading question: What is explained in the legend? Ryan: "How the loon got bad vocal folds." (How the loon's voice got so awful sounding) (captured by Rick and Ellyn)

Ryan's Quotes: Fourth Edition (2008-2009)

- "What did you do this weekend?" Ryan: "I was in doubt."

- How did you know that? Ryan: "By staring at the page and taking a quick glance."
- After Mrs. V (Ellyn) told him she would be waiting at the door after lunch... Ryan: "But I need you for social interaction."
- "I like politics. It's my favorite subject." What do you think about religion? Ryan: 'It's too complicated."
- After given choices of what to do.... "Blah, blah, blah."
- "What if my directions supersede the teacher's directions?"
- "I refuse to be taught by a teacher that makes mistakes."
- "School is too much for me!"
- Memorial Day writing: We are famous to honor the people that died and killed in the war. Before we do it though, remember this: Always cover your cough, wash your hands with soap and warm water, and don't spread germs to help prevent swine flu. Honoring these people that died in war: (list of people that died in war) Remember that.

We hope you have a great three day weekend!
God Bless America! Let Freedom Ring!
(captured by Rick and Ellyn)

The Spring of Ryan's fifth grade year, the students spent a few days at the North Cascades Institute. The students were asked to write about their experience and this was Ryan's rendering of his days in the Cascades.

Cascades
High in the snowy mountains
Brown and muddy
paths and trails
Dripping, wet fir trees
Colorful, pileated woodpeckers
near the narrow paths

Smells of stopping for lunch
of peanut-butter sandwiches
Boulders to climb over
Walking along
the gurgling, bubbling stream
Hearing the cascading, loud waterfall
Climbing a steep, rocky slope
Mountains

peaking through trees and clouds
Vision of the waterfall
for the first time
"Fantastic!"
Foaming, cascading water
rushing by me
Misty, cloudy weather
Opportunities to enjoy
beauty of the woods!

Ryan Cunningham©2010

Ryan's Quotes: Fifth Edition (2009-2010)

- Raised hand to answer a mental math problem. "I didn't get the answer because I didn't do the problem."
- "Mrs. V. (Ellyn) I will fill your brain with questions."
- "You force rules on me I can't even handle."
- Ran up to Mr. Bill (teacher) while he was teaching and asked, "Do you have a valid Washington State teaching credential?"
- During a free write Ryan wrote the start of *How The Grinch Stole Christmas*. When asked to share, he

stood in front of the class and recited half of the book without his writing in front of him.

- To a student teacher: "Don't be too hard on yourself today."

- Their writing assignment was to write about an important event in their life. Ryan wrote about the retirement of Charles Gibson.

- Students were asked to reorganize their data from a science experiment into a different format from the original. "This is torture! I'll just run in through the photo copier!"

- When asked what was the best part of Mountain School, he responded, "Taking exit 230 (home exit) off of I-5."

- After being sent to Mrs. D's room for inappropriate behaviors, Ryan wrote: "The truth of the matter is that you will always know what to do. The hard part is doing it." (H. Norman Schwarzkoph)

(captured by Rick and Ellyn)

Being Disabled

What is it like to be disabled?
Sometimes, you feel like the odd one out,

But then, sometimes, you don't – you feel quite happy!
(We all can be happy some way, without doubt)

However we appear, whatever we do,
Inside we're the same – but different, too!

So, I look upon others with pleasure and pride.
Don't make them feel hurt. Don't set them aside.
Love one another. Love everyone.
Because if you do, we'll all have lots of fun!

Ryan Cunningham © 2018

One final parting quote: My family took summer vacations to Folly Beach, S.C. for Ry's first seven birthdays. When he was three, we were standing at the surf's edge, the waves gently passing over our legs. As Ry looked east over the expansive Atlantic while the tide was rolling in, he turned to me and said, "*Moving mountains. The waves look like moving mountains.*" I got down on my knees to get his perspective... and he was spot on. As far as the eye could see, there were moving mountains headed to the shore.

Reeves/Cunningham

Shaving

The boy that would be a man, Ry, had entered puberty earlier than most of his peers, an early bloomer. He had always been on the tall side, but as a seventh and eighth grader, he towered over many of his classmates and quickly became acquainted with deodorant at my repeated and frequent requests and pleas. My man-child was definitely emotionally more child than man, but his body didn't care and he was revving into adolescence at light speed. By the time Ry was twelve, it was becoming apparent that he was going to have to learn to shave sooner than later. The cute peach fuzz he was acquiring was slowly beginning to resemble kudzu - invasive, never ending and out of control. I wasn't sure how to tackle this milestone, but figured being conservative and safe was the best route.

As a single Mom with no adult male energy in sight to guide him, I did the best I could and bought him a fancy-pants electric razor for Christmas. He wasn't super excited with the gift, it was just one step above new underwear and socks, but he did acknowledge that it seemed a better idea than a razor and I couldn't have agreed with him more. So, Braun in hand, we slowly worked over his fur-laden face and began the ritual of "manscaping". Ry seemed mostly okay with his bi-weekly ritual of facial restoration, but it did require a fair amount of reminders, cajoling and outright blackmail to get him to surrender to the electric razor. Over time, he began to lose enthusiasm for the chore. It slowly became a tug-of-war that was making the evening shower ritual around the household look like a grudge match.

One evening I asked him if there was a problem that I did not understand - I'm a little slow that way. Ry stood in front of me, twisting his ear (tic), and told me he didn't like the electric razor, that the noise and the way it pulled on his facial hair bothered him, and could he learn how to shave with a real razor? I stood in front of him, my mouth saying, "*Of course*", and my mind thinking, *"It's not my job to teach him, it should be his father's"*. As fate would have it, Ry and I were headed to Atlanta in a few weeks to take an extended family trip to Panama and we would be staying at my parent's home.

After Ryan had gone to bed, I was immediately on the phone to my father, "*Will you teach Ry to shave?*" My Dad didn't miss a beat. "*Of course, I'd be honored.*" So, with calendar in hand, I began to mark the days until we landed in Atlanta and my father could help my son with this rite of passage into manhood.

I am the youngest, by a solid decade, of three siblings. My parents had me in their mid-thirties and in turn, I had Ry in my mid-thirties. By the time Ry was thirteen, my father was squarely in his eighties. My father, a man of tradition and loyalty, was a career IBMer, a Mason and all around Southern gentleman by most accounts and my experiences. Ry adored him and I really couldn't think of a better man to teach my son how to navigate this new skill and the generational impact was not lost on me.

One evening after dinner, we all headed up to the "big bathroom" so that Dad could instruct Ry. I tried to stay out of the way, moving from the bath, to my mother's office, back to the bath. My father calmly began the process. First, the shaving cream needs to cover the entire surface. Ry was struggling with that... and my dad instructed him... "*No, you missed that spot...look in the mirror so that you can see...tilt your chin to see your neck...good, that's good!*" Ry, enraptured by his grandfather, followed directions, and did the best he could, which was pretty a-okay as far as I could tell.

Tears brimming in my eyes, I watched my father patiently explain to Ry the intricacies of shaving. How to go with the grain, against the grain, the best lines for the jaw, upper lip and Adam's apple... all the while, Ry staring into the mirror trying to mimic the instruction he was receiving, feeling stressed and empowered simultaneously. It was a transformative, generational moment - a passing of the torch and I felt honored to witness it. Tears and more tears later, I thanked my father and silently acknowledged the moment. Ry felt proud of his accomplishment and closer to his Granddaddy. All was well in the Reeves-Cunningham clan.

Over the next few months, Ry began to lose steam. He would miss the area under his sideburns, or neglect his neck. Oftentimes, it was bad enough that I would have to intervene and help him shave those areas, much to his chagrin. He was losing confidence, but was pushing against my entreaties of assistance - what teenager wouldn't? We were back to the tug of war of facial care and I was squarely losing the battle. After weeks of him flatly refusing to shave anything other than his chin and upper lip, we got into a control issue. I wanted him to shave properly, he wanted me to leave it up to him... back and forth, forth and back and his neck began to resemble the werewolf of London.

One particular evening Ry was resisting me with a vengeance and a worn out me was pushing back. His face needed attention and he was adamant to do it himself. Independence! After a full twenty minutes in the bathroom, his progress was about 5%, but he was dug in and resistant to receive input, especially from his Mom. I surrendered, knowing that it was a losing battle and trundled off to the bedroom for the night... I suppose it was around 9 p.m.

Sound asleep, a noise awakened me. As I roused awake, I saw flashes of disco-esque light cascading down my hallway towards my bedroom. Disoriented, I slammed out of sleep into the "*what the fc&@k*" place and tried poorly to reconcile my environs. What, better yet who, was in my house and what was going on? There was a loud rap on my opened bedroom door and I heard, "*Bellingham Police, ma'am, are you awake?*" "*Am I awake? I am now!*" Vaulting out of sleep, I sat up to see what was going on. I had a police officer in my house. Actually no, standing outside my bedroom door announcing himself. What in the hell was going on and why was this person in my home? I quickly rolled out of bed and asked the question, "*Why are you here?*" The officer apologetically told me that my son had called them. Standing in the hallway, half-asleep, I turned to the officer and said, "*He is autistic.*" And in return, the officer said, smiling, "*Yes, we figured that out.*"

As we walked down the hallway towards the living room, I asked why the police were in my home. The officer said that Ry had called them upset. "*Upset? About what?*", I asked. "*Did you all have an argument about shaving tonight?*" I stopped, trying not to laugh and said, "*Yea, we had a difference of opinion.*" The officer grinned and said Ry had called to report me about demanding that he shave and that he, the officer, was required to follow up, investigate and was sorry.

As we continued towards the living room, his partner, standing in front of Ryan, was describing how best to turn his (Ry's) chin to shave his neck and offered to show him in the bathroom. As Ry and the officer went into the bathroom, I turned to the first officer to apologize. He turned to me and smiled, "*Ma'am, this is the best call we have had all night.*" And so, Ry got a primer from the Bellingham Police Department and I again learned more about Ry's fears, my patience, parenting and humor!

[The next section was written by Ryan Cunningham.]

Shortly after the police arrived, Ryan Cunningham played--but not very well--"I'm Gonna Wash That Man Right Outa My Hair" (a song from South Pacific). This song is set in a situation where Ensign Nellie Forbush, who sings it, is almost fed up with her boyfriend Emile De Becque. Speaking of facial hygiene, Ryan's grandfather Donald Reeves, Sr., also taught Ryan how to shave.

Seizures and Surfing

When Ryan was eleven, he had his first seizures, back to back, two full on clonic tonics within 3 hours of each other. It was a typical evening, no precursor to the chaos that was to come shortly. My dear friend and Ry's after school nanny, Porcia, who had been living with us for a few months, was scheduled to be induced into labor for her first born that evening. She was terribly overdue and the doctors thought it best to hustle little Miss Avery along into this world. As I cooked dinner for Ry, Porcia, her husband, Chris, and her mother, Joyce, all vibrated along throughout the kitchen in anticipation of the impending birth. I was enjoying the celebratory moment with my extended family and eager to get my hands on this baby. It was a very loving and exciting evening as we told stories and laughed a lot, as was our practice.

As I served Ryan dinner, the rest of us orbiting around him and the kitchen, he suddenly went rigid. Joyce saw him first, turned to me and said, "*Mom*", pointing to Ryan! I grabbed Ry and slowly lowered him to the ground at about the moment that he began to convulse. Him turning blue, me going for a finger sweep and possible Heimlich, telling Porcia, Chris, anyone to call 911. Joyce keeping cool, Porcia freaking out and Chris making sure Porcia was okay. It was a bit surreal, definitely scary and seemed to last forever, but in reality, about sixty seconds. Ry limp and postictal, me wondering what the hell just happened and everyone else making sure Porcia did not go into labor in the kitchen!

The medics arrived lickety-split, assessed Ry and decided he needed to be transported to the emergency room to make sure everything was okay. Okay? Okay? I know these professionals in blue respond to seizures on a regular basis. But I was a neophyte, it was my son and suddenly things did not feel very "okay". They loaded Ry and me into the medic unit and we got a first class ride to the front of the line at our nearby hospital.

Ry was examined by a doctor and I was told that, although it is scary, a single seizure might be an isolated event, and we were sent home a couple of hours later with the Captain Obvious directions to keep a close eye on him. When we arrived home, it was close to bedtime and Ry was still exhausted. I put him to bed and parked myself outside his bedroom door. Couch cushions and a sleeping bag made for a great makeshift bed and I was prepared to sleep this way for days, weeks or months. I was frightened, very concerned and alone. Ten minutes into this new normal and Ry began to seize again. Grabbing my cell phone and leaping into Ry's bed, I called 911, simultaneously telling Ry that he was okay, things were going to be okay, he was safe and holding him loosely while his body shook.

Rinse and repeat, we were back in the medic unit, cruising to the hospital. This second seizure upped the ante and all of a sudden people were concerned and really paying attention. Upon our arrival at the emergency department, I asked if my friend Doctor Z. was on duty. You see, Joe has two autistic identical twins and knew my situation. A close family friend, he was a pediatrician by training, a trauma doc by passion and was in charge of this emergency department. As luck would have it, he was just punching out for the night, got my request and made a beeline to Ry and me. Exhausted, unsure and frightened for Ry, seeing Joe was like a window of hope and my sense of dread diminished ever so slightly.

Joe evaluated the situation, spoke to me about the seizures, conferred with his colleagues and Ry and I were scheduled for a med-flight to Seattle Children's Hospital. The source of the seizures was unknown, Bellingham did not have a pediatric neurologist and we were fast-tracked to the nearest available facility to make sure Ry did not have a brain bleed or other complications causing the seizure. Around 3 a.m., Ry and I were loaded into an ambulance, taken to the airport and placed onto a medically equipped plane headed south to Boeing Field. The nursing staff on the plane was attentive and amazing, helping me separate myself from the situation for a few minutes. Holding Ryan's left hand, I folded into myself, looked out at the inky darkness of the Puget Sound and repeated a small prayer... please let him be okay.

Upon arrival at Children's Hospital, Ry was immediately assessed, placed in a room, examined, examined again and for good measure, examined one more time. He was subjected to an EEG, MRI, blood work and cognitive tests over a three-day period. Diagnosis? Seizure Disorder! Prognosis? Unclear! Discharge instructions: no unsupervised baths, swimming alone was a no-no and the bicycle needed to be parked for six months. So, with seizure medications in hand, a new normal in front of us, relieved and simultaneously sad, we left Children's Hospital and headed home. Everything I (we) had worked steadily towards - short periods of independence, biking, and swimming, were gone in the blink of an eye and we needed to create a new rhythm in the household.

The first week or so after arriving home, I slept just outside Ryan's bedroom on the floor. Ry wasn't super excited about his loss of privacy, but I needed to be close, just in case. I researched seizure dogs, hired additional help around the house, purchased baby monitors and basically felt saddened and overwhelmed. What...what...what...were we going to do? While I was in hyper-driven, stressed out, find a solution Mom mode, Ry and I were scheduled to take a trip to Maui.

My close friend and Tai Chi teacher, Dani, and his wife, Anne, had moved to Maui the summer before. Him, a psychotherapist, her, a physician, had invited us over for a few days and we jumped at the opportunity to see them and visit Hawaii for the first time. We had purchased tickets in late October and had been looking forward to this adventure for a solid month. Now what? Doctor's orders: no water. Hawaii, all water. I felt confident that staying in the home of a physician in Hawaii was the best-case scenario for our situation. And so, the simple solution? Pack our bags, get on the plane and head southwest and see what happens.

The plane ride to Maui was remarkably stressful. I was walking on eggshells so to speak. After giving Ry his seizure and sleep meds, he got nauseated and vomited. We were midway over the Pacific, my son sick to his stomach, me in the bathroom rooting through his vomitus airsick bag looking for medication, and the flight attendants asking if we needed to turn back. We were halfway between the mainland and Hawaii, somewhere over the Pacific Ocean. It seemed that facing seizures in paradise with my friends for support was a better idea than turning the plane around and heading for the mainland with a planeload of angry vacationers. We landed in Hawaii, the rest of the flight being uneventful with me exhausted, but happy, and ready to enjoy our vacation.

Our first full day on the island was spent shopping and conspiring with our hosts. First stop, sporting goods store to purchase the most bomber life jacket known to humankind sold in Ry's size. Next phase, accommodation. How best to get Ry in the water safely? I wanted him to snorkel, swim and maybe surf, all the while being cognizant of the need to keep Ry safe. Solution? One SUP (stand up paddleboard) and two adults flanking one child. My friend, Dani, and I, sat on the shore under palm trees and problem solved every possible contingency. Once we felt confident that our plan was indeed safe, we put Ry on a stand up paddleboard, belly down, dive mask and snorkel equipped and us bracketing him. We floated with him five feet off shore over a small coral reef. Ry, lying on the board, was able to place his mask in the water and snorkel!!! It was genius and Ryan was thrilled. Score one for creativity!

Next challenge, surfing! There is a little pull-off-the-road park in Kihei. It is a shallow bay area, affectionately deemed Da Cove, that has perfect knee high waves on good days for novice surfers to learn the sport. The cove is mostly populated with would be, wanna be, has been surfers that like to hang out day after day, week after week, on the park benches, discussing the virtues of bygone surf and "talk story" of epic drops and rides. They are local color, interesting, caring and mostly harmless lost souls. As Dani and I unloaded boards, getting Ry suited up to ride waves, there was lots of talk about best lines, surf reports and cautionary tales from the locals; but the "boys" quickly recognized that our crew was different and they took us in like we were family, their own small ohana.

Heading out to the water, I got Ry on the surf SUP, hands and knees ready and began working our way out to the

"the surf". At the first decent wave, I turned the board, gave it a push and ran beside Ry, laughing and whooping it up as he hands-and-knees surfed to shore. That afternoon we made pass after pass, wave after small wave, until Ry grew weary and my legs would no longer function, sprinting through the knee high surf. The locals on the shore, hanging out drinking cheap beer and smoking weed, cheered our every success and gave Ry a solid fist pump after each wave, finally having a new story to talk about.

The rest of the trip was as expected for Maui - whale watching, the road to Hana, Haleakala, Lahaina banyan trees, Iao valley and more water time. With smiles stretching from ear to ear, Ry and I boarded our flight home feeling rejuvenated and ready to tackle the next phase of new challenges. We both learned that although his newly acquired seizure disorder was scary, it did not prevent us from leading an adventure filled life. It merely required that we pay close attention, plan for worst case scenarios and, once again, accept help from family and friends that wanted to support our journey. In the end, Ry has been pretty lucky in that his medications have kept most seizures at bay and he is able to enjoy most activities without restrictions.

As a final note, on Christmas morning Ry awakened with a full body rash. He was having a reaction to his seizure meds and was headed toward Steven Johnson's Syndrome. As luck would have it, the E.R. doc on duty, Walt, was a veteran to emergency medicine, had a very strong personality, and was a good listener. As he and I discussed Ry's meds, he researched Trileptal and discovered it was the culprit. As he headed down the hall to call Children's Hospital for a consult, I asked him to find the oldest med used for treating seizures. I did not want a "boutique" medication that double-dipped as a mood stabilizer or something else. I wanted a medicine with the sole purpose of quelling seizures and had been field tested for decades. Long story, not so short, after a very long coming to terms with the resident on duty down south in Seattle, Walt called in a script for a simple old-school med and we never had another issue.

Electronics

I'm not sure which came first, Ry's uncanny, savant behaviors with all things electronic or his unwavering obsessive fixation with user's manuals and the *For Dummies* instructional book series. By the time Ry turned the corner from kindergarten to first grade, he was displaying ninja skills with basic electronic devices and had homing pigeon accuracy finding cell phones, remotes and computers that had not been "secured" by the owner. Ry took advantage of every opportunity to explore, test and crash any piece of technology he could get his little fingers around. For about three years I did everything within my power to keep him away from stores like Best Buy. If I had to go, his little nervous system would be scattered and shattered into a thousand pieces, as he would sprint to and fro throughout the store - frantically racing up and down the aisles of the computer section trying out any device that was available for demo. Extricating him, a super human feat, usually ended up with him screaming and thrashing around while I gently put him over my shoulder and carried him out the door. One or two of those experiences and stores like Best Buy and Radio Shack were placed on our do not fly list.

It's hard to describe the extent of Ry's superhero powers. I had never seen anything akin to it and it happened so fast that it seemed sleight of hand. If it weren't for the obvious triage needed to resurrect devices, I would doubt that my wunderkind was responsible for these incidences. The most difficult part was convincing people that my cute, tow-headed, little sidekick could indeed deep six their bits and pieces of programmable silicon. No device was immune and my parents were going to discover this in short order and the hard way.

The first seven years of Ry's life, my family would meet up in Atlanta in July and caravan to the Low Country, the barrier-islands off the coast of Charleston, for a large puppy pile family vacation. Ry and I would typically arrive in Atlanta a couple of days beforehand so that we could have some travel downtime and not have to suffer back-to-back epic travel days. It seemed a good practice and gave my folks some focused, quiet time with their youngest grandson before the rest of the Reeves clan landed on their doorstep.

Every time we came back to Atlanta for a visit, there was a steep learning curve while my parents got their bearings around Ryan's needs and difficulties. I would try to coach them before our arrival, but it wasn't as helpful as spending some quiet time with us at the house. On one particular summer trip back to Atlanta, Ry swept into my parent's house, a category 4 hurricane the likes of which would have startled the most seasoned FEMA veteran. Against my repeated warnings and decrees of doom and danger, my parents had not secured ALL of their devices and had no comprehension of the damage Ry could impart in the blink of an eye. They were proverbial lambs to slaughter.

Round One: BlackBerry vs. Ry:

The first victim to fall was an innocent BlackBerry, minding it's own business, nestled on the coffee table, between magazines, in the family room. Ryan spotted the phone out of the corner of his eye, turned on his heel, and immediately traversed the room. With his eyes fixed on the prize, legs pumping with excited determination, he grabbed the phone before any of us could react. I was up immediately grabbing the phone from Ry, but it was too late. Within seconds, and I mean less than ten, Ry had managed to disable the phone. As I passed the phone to my father, I apologized knowing full well that saying "*I told you so*" wasn't going to be well received by him.

My father looked at the phone, touched a couple of the keys, looked at me and said, "*What in the hell did he do to my phone?*" Ry had managed to lock my father out of his device. More to the point, he locked down the device completely, making it unusable. At this point, Ry was incredibly upset because his hard won prize had been relinquished, my father was rattled because his business phone had been compromised and I sat there trying, with limited success, to mollify both aggrieved parties.

Phone clutched in hand, my father disappeared to his basement office to phone BlackBerry technical support. After a lengthy conversation and failed attempts at recovery, the gentleman on the other end of the line surrendered and hoped my father had saved his contacts. I always wondered if the people at BlackBerry ever considered that a six year old had easily destroyed the same phone used by POTUS.

Round Two: Microwave vs. Ry

After Ry laid waste to the phone, everyone decided to batten down the hatches. My father made sure the basement door leading to his office remained closed and locked. My mother, not to be outdone, turned off her laptop, hid it under seat cushions and closed her office door, hoping that a shut door would not be inviting to her grandson. Everyone breathed a sigh of relief and tried to put the incident behind them.

As was my habit when I returned to my parent's home, I went for a run around the old neighborhood. I always enjoyed jogging the old familiar routes and seeing how things had changed here and there while I had been away. On rare occasion, I would see people I knew and take the time to chat and catch up on the past twenty years. As my parent's child, stopping was expected and as I aged, I had grown to enjoy these southern social invasions during my runs.

As I was headed out the door, my mother told me to take my time and enjoy, that she and Ry would be fine. For whatever reason, I firmly held onto that belief and cruised down the driveway. Upon returning from "Kim-time", I found Mom and Ry in the kitchen. Paula was putting away lunch and Ry was playing with the microwave. I stopped, looked and asked Ry to stop. My mother assured me that everything was fine and she had been "supervising" him. Right!

Later that day, as my mother headed back into the kitchen to start supper, I heard, "*Don, come here!*" That's never a good thing. My mother had discovered something that she was uncomfortable with and wanted my father's assistance. As he walked into the kitchen, with me close on his heels, she pointed to the microwave. As far as I could tell, the appliance seemed intact and functioning; however, the display wasn't in English any more. In fact, on first glance, it appeared to be in a language that I did not recognize. As my mother's stress level began to rise, I fetched Ry and asked him to fix the micro.

Ry knew something was wrong, that he was the cause and he became very stressed and collapsed within himself. Under the pressure of three adults begging him to fix the microwave and on the heels on the Blackberry massacre, he shut down and flatly declared that he could not. Okay, take a deep breath and let's all take a step back and problem solve. First up, find the owner's manual. While my mother and father were digging through files to find the directions, I was checking out the display. For whatever reason, it occurred to me/us that Ry had programmed it to display Portuguese. No problem, let's go to the language section and figure out how to program it back to English.

Well, according to the book, the microwave could only be programmed for Spanish, French, German and English - Portuguese was not an option. It may have been about that time that my father poured a scotch for himself and gin and tonics for the rest of us. We decided to sit in the family room and take a break. While the adults were busy with their pre-dinner, can we manage this, what's next, cocktail hour, Ryan sneaked back into the kitchen and re-programmed the microwave back into English.

And so began a new found universal respect and awe for Ry's ability to navigate the electronic world. As a cautionary note, if he comes for a visit, hide the remotes!

[This section is written by Ryan Cunningham]
I started using computers at a young age. Over time I have taught myself the Bourne Shell language, C, C++, and Python. I am particularly interested in Linux-based open source operating systems like Fedora, Debian, Ubuntu and GNU. It is fun for me to find programming bugs and send the developers patches to fix the problems whenever possible. I have recently translated a Sugar Labs internal communication into Spanish. It relates to the closure of stage 3 of elections for their Oversight Board. I would like to do more Spanish translations for Sugar Labs and other companies.

Too Many Puzzle Pieces

Executive Functions: a collection of cognitive skills that allow flexible thinking so that we can organize, plan and achieve goals. There are several skills that we acquire over time and with practice; some individuals with autism struggle with the following skills:

1. Impulse or inhibitory control: the ability to think before acting.
2. Emotional control: the ability to keep emotions in check.
3. Flexible thinking: the ability to adjust to the unexpected.
4. Working memory: the ability to store key information.
5. Self-monitoring: the ability to evaluate how you're doing.
6. Planning and prioritizing: the ability to decide on a goal and create a plan to meet it.
7. Task initiation: the ability to take action and get started.
8. Organization: the ability to keep track of things physically and mentally.

Information liberally taken and poorly paraphrased from *Wikipedia* and *Understood.org*[6]

What it is like to raise a child with impaired executive functions? It took my son fifteen years to learn how to cross the street safely. Years and years of coaching for him to:

1. Stop
2. Look both ways
3. Look again
4. Make a determination
5. Take appropriate action
6. Cross safely

It may seem like a simple task, but for my Ry it was synonymous with crossing the Grand Canyon by tightrope. Initially, he could not decide where the perimeter or the boundaries of the intersection began. This is not an

---

[6] From *Wikipedia*.

<http://en.wikipedia.org/w/index.php?title=Executive_functions&old id=768476726> (last modified 2017-03-04T01:09Z). From *Understood.org.* <http://www.understood.org/en/learning-attention-issues/child-learning-disabilities/executive-functioning-issues/key-executive-functioning-skills-explained> (no date of creation or last modification given). Both articles accessed on 2017-03-11T08:16—08:00. Footnote added by Ryan Cunningham.

unusual issue for most little people, but as Ry entered middle school, he was not sorting the information clearly and that's way outside of norms. Frequently, he would stand ten feet from the corner without a clear street view or plant himself a couple feet into the road not attending to the margins of the sidewalk. After lots of coaching and years of repetition, in eighth grade Ryan began to get the geographical hang of intersections, but that was only step one in our six step series.

The next obvious hurdle was to look both ways and make a decision about traffic. He was pretty good at looking up and down the road, but I did not have confidence that he was actually seeing the road or better yet, the cars. It was a rote movement that took place so quickly, right, left, right, left, never settling into one direction or the other for any meaningful amount of time - the entire process completed in ten seconds or less. It seemed damned near impossible to me that he was tracking vehicles very well, and frankly, I could not understand how he didn't get vertigo.

Once I got him to slow down and really look, the last step, make a decision, stymied him for years. We would be on bikes, waiting on traffic, Ry watching, watching, and watching some more. After the road was totally clear, there would be about a twenty second delay before he would tell me it was safe to cross. Okay, that was a true statement twenty seconds ago, but by the time he processed the information and decided to take action, it was too late, more traffic had arrived. It could take us a solid five to ten minutes to get across a minor, but moderately trafficked intersection.

I will never forget the day Ry mastered "the intersection" and crossed with the ease befitting a pro. It was a spring afternoon in 2016 and I had the luxury of working from home that day. I had turned my comfy chair around to face the window so that I could grade papers in the sun and occasionally watch critters move about the garden. As I sat there, taking a break from student papers, I saw Ry's school bus scoot by and deposit him a block or so from the house. As Ryan headed up the sidewalk, he came to the cross- roads and stopped. He looked both ways, didn't miss a beat and crossed safely! Truth be told, it was my soccer Mom moment. I was so excited! Ry had finally "gotten it" and I breathed a sigh of relief knowing this opened a brand new door for his independence.

Ry struggles with all eight categories of executive functioning skills.

1. Impulse Control: Ry began struggling with impulse control when he entered pre-school. This was his first social experience around a lot of children. A typical day in the classroom might begin with him having to see **everything** in the room - dashing from desk to desk, bookshelf to computer, to the teacher's desk and back again, over and over, 'the circuit'. And if there were a singular change, he would find it in nanoseconds. Ry upset because he couldn't successfully sort out the differences in his environs. Behaviors might then escalate with Ryan having an idea or thought in the middle of a lesson or activity. He might jump up, race to part of the classroom, grab a book, taking an eraser, and try to get computer access. And his teacher wondering what was happening, slightly shell shocked and struggling to maintain order.

On a typical day, Ry could do this hundreds of times and if he was denied his routine, he would throw himself on the ground, dead weight, refuse to cooperate and declare that his teacher and aides needed to be fired. The school tried interventions such as a weighted vest to help him feel grounded and slow him down, and time-out walks up and down the halls and outdoors, but all to no avail. After seven years of Ry's extreme impulsivity, I finally surrendered and placed him on medications when he entered fifth grade. He was getting older, bigger, and more unpredictable. I needed help to smooth out his nervous system so that he could manage himself better. The medications were not 100% victorious, but provided just enough biochemical support so that Ry could function better as he began to slam into puberty and all of the horrors of that hormonal upheaval. As a side note, for years I had resisted the notion of medicating my child. The entire idea was abhorrent to me. I was adamant that he did not need pharmaceuticals for optimal function. In this particular case I was dead wrong! I harbored regret for a number of years because, by not having a more open mind, I had not provided the best care for my child.

2. Emotional control: Emotional control was not part of the household vernacular until Ry turned sixteen. Up until that point, Ry's emotional status could resemble a typical weather pattern in early spring-- unsettled, unpredictable, and quickly changing with very little warning. His limbic system was in overdrive and dictated that most of his emotional responses were somewhere on the moderate to extreme scale. He had complete emotional dysregulation and that got in the way of him participating fully in the classroom. He was frequently pulled out of class because of an outburst and his inability to self-modulate his

behaviors. Once he entered middle school, the severity and frequency of his outbursts were becoming problematic, a product of more complex class schedules and hormonal flux. The first time he received in-school suspension, I had an overwhelming sense of despair. Ry was a wonderful child, but his lack of emotional control, regardless of his IEP, was getting him in trouble. The second time he was suspended, I met with the Assistant Principal and said, *"Ann, you can make us or break us. Ry is a good kid and I need your help. We cannot survive middle school without your support."* She looked at me, said *"Okay,"* and immediately became our champion, giving us the boost we needed to get Ry though his worst behavioral period. Without that administrative help, Ry would have never succeeded in middle school and I am forever thankful that he was no longer defined by his outbursts.

As Ry matured, he got better at self-regulation and de-escalation. He still has outbursts now and again, the frequency increasing when he is stressed or frustrated, but in the big scheme of things, he was no more dramatic than many of his classmates. However, he lacked the social filter to understand exactly how his outbursts were/are received by onlookers.

3. Flexible thinking: Ry has very little flexible thinking. Most days, if there is an event, action, activity he has not predicted, he asks, "*What is happening?*" He is simply not able to sort out the unexpected. If, for instance, we are driving to a particular destination (and by the way, my son has uncanny navigation skills, which makes travel fun) and there is an accident, construction or whatnot and we are caught in traffic, Ry cannot tease out what is happening in that situation. I can explain to him that it may be an accident or a stalled car, but he cannot get his head wrapped around why we have to be stalled in traffic. And to compound the situation, if I decide to take an alternate route, Ry becomes increasingly upset because he has the expectation to go from point A to point B in an earlier prescribed path. To deviate from his expectations is difficult for him to process and accept. A lack of flexible thinking can cause an individual to have a very rigid view of day to day happenings and sometimes they get stuck in the proverbial "my way or the highway". In other words there is a correct and an incorrect way of doing things - very black and white thinking. It may not be difficult for the person lacking flexible thinking but it can be exhausting for loved ones living with them.

4. Working memory: Ry's lack of working memory has been a constant and consistent source of problems for him at home and school. I don't even know that I can clearly describe what it is like. Let's say Ry misses the bus after school. He has a perfectly functioning cell phone and could easily call me to come get him but he doesn't. It does not occur to my son to call and ask for a ride, but instead he walks the five or so miles to our house shouldering a thirty- pound book bag. When he gets home, if I ask why he didn't call, he simply says, "*I don't know*" while twisting his ear, stressed by the perceived judgment that he made a mistake.

One day I came home from work and Ry was just leaving the bathroom and the tub was draining. I can't remember the last time I saw Ry take a bath (pre-seizure days) and asked what's up. He explained that he was cold and decided to take a warm bath. Noting that he was dressed in shorts and a t-shirt, I asked if he had thought to put on a sweatshirt? "*No*", he had not considered that. Then I asked if he had considered turning up the heat on the thermostat? Once again, "*No*". And finally I said, " *Ry, if you were cold enough to take a hot bath, why are you back in your shorts and t-shirt*"? He simply responded, "*I do not know.*" He was not able to problem solve and that is a deficit in working memory.

Additionally, do not ask a person with poor working memory to perform more than one task at a time. If I am heading out the door to run errands and ask Ry to empty the dishwasher before I return home, (one step direction) there is about a 60% chance that he will begin the task before I return. However, if I tell him to empty the dishwasher, make his bed and brush his teeth (3 step direction) there is a 0% chance that anything will be completed. Giving Ry multiple-step directions causes him to functionally shut down. His brain cannot sort through the perceived "multi-tasking" and therefore he forgets what it was he was supposed to complete.

School is another "granimal" all together. Ry's teachers do a good job of posting homework assignments on the whiteboard at the head of class. Ry understands that the information is there and when arriving to class he needs to write down the information to bring home so that he can complete the assignment. For any other student, this may seem an easy task. But for Ry, nothing could be more complex. Let me try to break it down.

1. Ry goes into the classroom surrounded by 30+ other students. Lots of stimuli: teenagers pushing, laughing, chairs scraping against the floor and everyone hustling to get to their seats, the bell rings.

2. Upon arriving he needs to find a way to filter out everything else (see #1) and look to the whiteboard to find the assignment.

3. He doesn't have good peripheral vision processing, therefore, if he is not standing or seated directly in front of the posted assignment, (and often teachers post in the upper corner of the board) he may not see it and will not remember to look for it. Out of sight, out of mind.

4. If he is fortunate enough to discover the note on the whiteboard, he has to maintain enough focus to pull out his notebook and record the information before being distracted by verbal directions being given by his instructor. Ry also struggles with task initiation and may become frozen in place if he is trying to balance two tasks, not knowing which to do first and, therefore doing nothing.

5. Then 4 hours later, when he gets home and settled in to do schoolwork, he has to:

    a. Remember he had homework assigned

    b. Look for it and find it in his book bag

    c. Stay focused enough to complete it

   6. If he is able to complete the first 5 steps, then he has to remember to turn in the material to his teacher, and that may be a class that he only attends three days a week. The time gap becomes insurmountable in his ability to attend appropriately and recall anything substantive.

And so, these are the primary reasons my son's GPA dropped a solid grade point since he lost his in-class instructional aide. Ry does not have the working memory to consistently complete these tasks and it negatively impacts him as a student.

5. Self-monitoring: I can only remember a handful of times when I have asked Ry how he was doing and his response was anything other than, "*I'm doing great!*" As a little guy, when he was upset and crying, I would ask him if he was happy and every single time he would answer "*yes*". It's not that Ry is/was clueless about his emotive spaces; he just can't easily tease out how he is feeling from how he wants to be feeling. There is a fine distinction in that statement. His inability to self-monitor also extends into peer relationships, school achievement, physicality, and basic

social skills -- like using your inside voice and whispering when you are trying to have a quick exchange during a movie instead of blurting out, "*I have to go to the bathroom*". It doesn't occur to Ry that:

> 1. He is being loud in a space that requires quiet discretion and
>
> 2. Telling everyone in the movie theater that he has to go to the bathroom is a social faux pas.

This inability to self-monitor has gotten in the way of him making social connections with his peers. Most of the kids in his school are remarkably sweet and kind to him, but do not invite him to gatherings and activities because they do not know how to wrangle his behaviors.

6. Planning and prioritizing: Ry has very little ability to plan and prioritize information and it impacts him academically. He has very little concept of setting a goal and then the step-by-step process of reaching that goal. I refer to it as magical thinking when he says he is going to do "x" and I ask him how he is going to achieve that? And then there is absolute silence. We may sit down and work through all of the steps that need to occur, but he rarely initiates them (see skill 7 below). We work on this frequently, but in truth, I don't get too concerned about

this deficit. I am a college professor and the vast majority of my students still struggle with this skill set.

7. Task initiation: This ability has always been predicated upon fixations. If Ry wanted to create a new operating system for his computer, learn a new Broadway musical piece, or memorize a Wikipedia page, then task initiation was not a problem. Ryan's difficulty would be going for a run. It would be heavy lifting for him to transition from the house to the trail. Figuring out appropriate clothes, and where and when to run, could take up the better part of a Sunday afternoon, most times ending with him never getting out the door because the planning and the execution was too much to process and therefore he shuts down. When he was younger he had job boxes to help him organize step-by-step processes, but truthfully, they didn't help him much.

During his eleventh grade IEP meeting, his Special Education teacher presented IEPs from 1st, 5th, 8th grades etc. It was a profoundly sad moment for me. One of the goals on each IEP was one form or another of task initiation and organization. Right there, in black and white, it was apparent that Ry had not improved or made progress in regards to this deficit.

The good news is that he has finally turned a corner on this skill. Given enough reminders, Ry will get out of his stasis and follow through on a task about 50% of the time. It helps me keep a glass half full attitude.

8. Organization: Find me a teenager that never loses anything and I will introduce you to the next POTUS[7]. My son's room looks like a bomb exploded within. Okay, maybe an exaggeration, but there are piles of books, papers, maps - you name it - all over the place. I suppose if the space were tidier it would be easier for him to organize his life. However, there is a valid reason I allow his room to maintain this level of disarray. Ry is a little obsessive, compulsive. Actually, he is moderately OCD. When we go to the grocery store, he will naturally and quite spontaneously straighten the items on the shelves. Every item equally spaced and labels facing perfectly forward. I don't think he realizes he is doing it. As he walks by a boxes of food, if one is out of place, he will fix it without missing stride. When he was a little person, he would love going with me to work. His favorite thing was to be left alone in the faculty support office so that he could organize pens, pencils, binder clips, etc. (remember the ball pit story?) At home he makes sure all of the glasses in the

---

[7] *POTUS:* President of the United States.

cabinet are aligned in a certain fashion and that the bathroom towels are hung properly, rules that I don't quite understand, but accommodate. Ry comes by these traits quite honestly and I recognize that they are important to him. His father had compulsivity to the point of disabling. I think Lee was trying to control his environment so that he could minimize the unexpected. I don't think that is Ry's end goal, but it may be. All I know is that if he chooses to keep his room a mess, I don't interfere with the process provided it doesn't create a public safety hazard in the house.

In the end, lacking executive functions skills will continue to impact Ry into adulthood. He will most likely never drive. His inability to quickly decide and adapt to the ever-changing patterns of traffic and unpredictability of other drivers will keep him from sitting behind the wheel of a car. He will require much needed support to manage the most basic college class having not yet mastered the abilities to organize information and remember key information. And living independently? I hope so, only because he wants that for himself.

Problem Solving

I have always been drawn to old stuff, plain and simple.
Growing up in the South, there was always an over
abundance and wealth of old, interesting, "cool" things
(some might say junk) at hand for someone like me. Go to
any yard sale and you will find complete sets of
Wedgewood china or antique pieces that families are
desperate to get out of their attics and basements. It is a
cornucopia of horse glue and tiger oak chest of drawers,
tarnished flatware and the occasional dented pewter
pitcher - generations of use and neglect telling stories
across the surfaces of family pieces and relics.

When I moved across the country, I was judicious about
what items made the journey. I packed a few antiques that
belonged to no one I knew, purchased at an antique mall
in Marietta or Alpharetta, Georgia. But mostly, I brought
family pieces with me. My parent's first dining table, my
paternal great-grandfather's hand tools, a jewelry box and
doll chest made by my maternal great-grandfather, some
sterling silver baubles and a simple retro, 1950's Zenith
radio that my parents once used. My mother begged me to
take more of my things (again, insert junk) with me to the

Pacific Northwest, but I simply replied that I would get them later.

Over time, I framed the tools in a rough- hewn shadow box, refinished the dining table, filled the jewelry box and doll chest, but never did anything with the radio. Much to my sadness, the old Zenith didn't work. Over its lifetime, my father had replaced the plug, but it no longer produced sound, its innards giving up the ghost a number of decades past. It was just Film Noir cool enough that I kept it on a shelf in my reading room, a reminder of family and simpler times that I could barely recall. Eventually, I gave up on it and stored it away in a closet, vowing to get it repaired one day.

It's funny how a singular decision, benign in design, can impact your life, take your breath away and leave you in stunned silence, trying to put together the pieces of the world you once understood. One day, a Friday, February, in 2014, I decided to get the Zenith fixed. I was going to take it to the local radio museum, Sparks, and see if they could recommend a craftsman to repair it. I imagined it on my kitchen countertop, NPR playing from it while having my morning coffee. Per usual, I placed the radio on the hearth and left it there for weeks, procrastinating - a reminder to get it done, but in no real hurry. During that time span, Ry never once gave the Zenith a second glance. He never asked about it, picked it up, or looked at it as far as I could ascertain.

On March 13th, a Friday no less, Ry had an early release day from school. He was home by 11 a.m. I had arranged for him to have lunch with an ex-boyfriend. They were to meet at 11:45 or so and head out the door, hunting for food, doing the "guy" thing. I had to teach class from 11:30 to 1:00 and then I could be home with Ry for the rest of the afternoon. It was a perfect solution to the craziness of the school district's early release calendar.

As I was calling class roll, I received a text, "*Ry has had a seizure, he is okay*". Okay? Okay? No, he is not okay! My son had never had a break through seizure. I looked at the text, looked at my students and said, "*Class is cancelled*" and made a beeline to the house. Upon arriving home, I found Ry disoriented, nauseated, and asking to sleep. Medics were attending to him. They were discussing the seizure, his possible postictal state and asking if I wanted him transported to the hospital. As I was talking with them and listening to Ry, I noticed that he was slurring his S's. I turned to the medics and said, "Transport him now!", and we were off to the E.R., again.

In my late twenties I decided to volunteer for Bellingham Mountain Rescue Council, the technical side of Search and Rescue in Whatcom County. We would head into the Cascades to find missing and injured climbers, look for Alzheimer walk-away patients, and recover bodies from avalanche and crevasse deaths. We were a tight knit bunch of skilled outdoorsy dirt bags serving Whatcom County and trusted each other implicitly.

As Ryan was wheeled into an examination room, the E.R. doc, a familiar face, walked into the room. We had served together on Mountain Rescue for a solid five+ years and he was the best thing I had seen in days. Jeff immediately assessed the situation, asking questions, talking to Ry and quickly ordered a CT scan.

As I stood in the examination room, quiet and deep in thought, I began to wonder what had happened. I wasn't convinced Ryan experienced a seizure; there was no evidence to support that notion. It was apparent that he had some type of brain event because he wasn't tracking well, complained of tiredness and a headache, but not a seizure. The clock ticked away, my brain wanting answers and all I could do was wait for the CT results.

Approximately 30 minutes later, Ry was wheeled back into the room and shortly after, Jeff returned with the results. Ryan had fractured his skull and had a brain bleed. He had paged the neurosurgeon and Ryan was scheduled for surgery as soon as the surgeon arrived. There was lots of chatter: do you understand what's happening, can you sign this form of consent, we need to open him up stat, does he have medication allergies, etc, etc.? I looked at Jeff and Barry (the surgeon) and said, "*Do it... now!*"

The long and short of the story is that Ry was in surgery for about two hours. He had fractured his skull in the temporal region and thankfully, only had a small epidural bleed (not subdural bleed) that was more easily repaired. As I got the post-surgical report from the surgeon, I took a deep breath, thanked him and headed to the ICU. Ry and I spent a solid four days in the ICU and another day or so in the MCU (Medical Care Unit). It was an exhausting period of limited sleep, marginal food, and lots of advocacy, but I was grateful he was healing and the injury was less severe than originally thought. I slowly watched Ry physically improve, but emotionally falter.

On the second day in the I.C.U., I took an hour or so to race home and get some essentials - clean clothes, toothbrush, kindle, etc. As I walked towards my front door, I decided to tease out what had happened - a little detective work. He had fractured his skull, okay, but how? Ry was found just outside the front door. It was assumed he had a seizure, fell on to the concrete porch and injured himself. As I approached the front door, I found no evidence of this story. Where he landed, I would have expected a mess in the pea gravel and beauty bark that flanks my small stoop, him thrashing around in the throes of a clonic/tonic seizure, but there was nothing. I sat on the porch and wondered what, what had happened, willing Ry to point me in the right direction.

As I went inside, I looked all over the kitchen and living room to see if I could find damage, any indication where he may have hit his head. As I walked through the kitchen, I noticed the Zenith radio, on the kitchen countertop, partially plugged into the outlet! I stood there and stared at the radio and slowly things came into focus. Ry got the radio and plugged it in. Something must have happened and he tried to unplug it, but it had a bad plug and wouldn't easily dislodge. What happened? How did Ry injure himself? Talk to me Ry!

I began to put myself in Ryan's shoes and tried to fit together the puzzle pieces of what could have occurred. After a day or so of working things through my head, I had a fairly good idea of what may have happened but needed Ryan to confirm. It took weeks for his memory of that event to return and Ry finally explained to me what had happened on that fateful day. When he plugged in the radio, he heard a pop. He tried to unplug the Zenith but it wouldn't cooperate. Ry immediately believed he was in danger of electrocution - not necessarily a bad thought on his part - but he believed the entire house was charged with electricity and he would be killed. His response was fight or flight and he sprinted out of the kitchen, tripped and slammed his head into a wall, fracturing his skull, concussing his brain, and producing an epidural brain bleed. When he came to, he still believed he was in danger, got up, dragged himself out the front door, passed out and concussed himself again on the patio and that is where he was found.

It is hard to know if this event would have occurred if Ry was not autistic and struggling with executive functions. I can process, reprocess and think about this a thousand times, but it is meaningless. There is no way to know for sure.

155

What I do know about this event is that Ry was seriously impacted from his injuries. A few weeks later he had his first break through seizure. He was finally old enough to realize that the head injuries and seizure seemed scary and that he was no longer an immortal teenager. His anxiety and insecurity increased to the point of paralysis at times and he began to really doubt his ability to live independently.

We always talk about one step forward, two steps back, but in this circumstance, it was a minimum of ten steps back. Everything changed. Ry doubted himself and I worried incessantly whenever he was home alone. He wasn't tracking very well and had extreme cognitive fatigue. Each school day was a struggle and very exhausting to him. In a period of one year his G.P.A. dropped a full point, and he regressed emotionally and academically.

It has been three plus years since his injury. Things have changed and we are at a new normal. Ry is a lot more conservative about taking chances and, of course, I am always concerned but reticent whenever he is home alone. I am thankful that he is making progress and that the incident wasn't more life altering. I firmly believe that he still struggles with major post-concussive issues that have impacted him academically, socially and that his working memory deficits have increased. But he seems to be improving and that's all this mom can hope for.

Pegasus

Ry began middle school in seventh grade, sort of. Like every other fifth grader living in the downtown core of our hometown, Ry didn't have a middle school to attend. The year before his sixth grade year, in an attempt to update earthquake safety, the aged middle school went through an exhaustive retrofit to insure that the building met basic safety standards. One evening, late, a spark from a welder's torch inadvertently landed in an inopportune place, smoldering undetected for hours. As the wind increased throughout the night, a fire erupted into a three engine disaster, the building gutted by flames.

As neighbors, families and friends gathered, in shock, gawking, crying, hugging, everyone wondered the same thing - where will the students go to school next year? The school district, scrambling, created an action plan and the kids were farmed out to different schools scattered across our small town. And so, Ry was bussed, seven miles, to an elementary school that had space to house a bunch of rowdy sixth graders. No one was really happy with the circumstances, but everyone managed, kind of, and the children and staff limped through the school year as best they knew how.

The local construction company that was contracted to fix the burned out mess worked like fiends and put contractors and sub-contractors on the site 24 hours a day. They were hell bent on rebuilding the school in time for the next school year and, miraculously, they succeeded. So Ryan, as a seventh grader, walked through the doors of his newly built, rebuilt middle school, eager to begin this new journey.

I have always tried to be involved at my son's school. I didn't have the home situation or job that gave me license to volunteer in his classroom, but I was engaged with his teachers, staff and administration. Any chance I had to volunteer after-hours, I was there excited to participate. One afternoon, while in the school office waiting to pick up Ry, I noticed a reader board in the corner. On the screen there were a variety of announcements scrolling across my periphery and I noticed something that piqued my interest - Running Club. His middle school had a running club that met four days a week after school! I had been looking for an activity or club Ryan could participate in, seeking inclusion and integration with his new gaggle of peers, and this club had potential.

Ry could run, sort of, and I could help, mostly. I contacted the teacher that was the lead for this club and Robert enthusiastically encouraged Ry's participation. Robert saw past Ryan's disability and welcomed him to the group.

After the first few weeks, we fell into a comfortable pattern. I would show up a couple afternoons a week and run with the kids, providing support for Ry and filling my heart spaces with happiness. After three or four weeks, Robert mentioned that the kids were going to have a meet with a local middle school and could I run with Ry? There was concern that, because of Ry's slow speed, and gravitational insecurity issues, he would be left behind and maybe get lost. I was more than a little bit excited to run side-by-side with my son while he explored this new passion and agreed whole-heartedly to accompany him.

There are a number of anecdotes I can offer with regard to this first year of athletics, but I will mention just one. I believe it was our third and last meet of the season. Whatcom Middle School (Ry's school) was running against Shuksan Middle School. The meet was to take place at a local park closer to the other school - an away meet. This particular course was challenging for Ry because of numerous very steep and muddy descents. His gravitational insecurity turned to fear and he needed lots of coaxing and hand holding to get down those hills. In a word, we were slow. The fastest kid on the course, from the opposing school, had crossed the finish line a solid ten+ minutes ahead of my son. As Ry neared the finish line, the last athlete on the course, I stopped running and told him to finish the race on his own. As I stood in the distance, tears streaming down my face, so proud of his accomplishment, there, at the finish line was the Shuksan runner. He was waiting to cheer on my son. I don't think most people knew how physically hard it was for Ry to run. He wasn't like the other kids, he didn't have the physicality to easily cruise through these activities. The athlete from Shuksan acknowledged that with his presence. He congratulated Ry, told him "Good race"! And that's when I fell in love with cross-country, its athletes and coaches.

Over the next six years, Ryan continued his participation in cross-country and I supported him on almost every race. It was a gift for me to be able to run side-by-side with my son watching him struggle, grow, succeed and find connections amongst his prep athlete peers. I was able to better understand his mindset. He wasn't interested in being "competitive", he just wanted to run because he loved it so. This, by the way, was a good lesson for his oh-so-competitive mother. He capturing joy in the experience, not the outcome of the race, was a great life lesson for everyone. It also gave me hope for this generation of young adults. True to form, at the completion of every race, his teammates and opponents would wait for him to cross the finish line, cheering him on and giving exuberant high fives. I was never able to walk away from a race without tears and gratitude for this community and its loving kindness towards my son.

Happy Birthday to You

I am not sure when I decided to call it our tradition, but Ryan had his first birthday trip when the family celebrated his first cycle around the sun. My parents generously rented a sprawling, ramshackle beach house on Folly Island in South Carolina and it was there the family embraced his birth. He had no idea why everyone was so excited, clapping, singing, carrying on and gushing over him, but he was thrilled with the blue icing on his cake, getting more on his face than in his mouth and the party and vacation were deemed a success.

From that point forward Ry and I always spent his birthdays on the road, adventuring, getting into mischief and thoroughly enjoying aliveness. The first seven years were Reeves family caravans to Folly. We would puppy pile together, cousins playing in the surf, grandparents watching from the sleeping porch, parents drinking cheap beer and trying to keep up with the kids without inflicting permanent damage on aging bodies. It was a raucous, fun and sometimes, irreverent time, but as the grandchildren began having their own babies, the tradition came to an end.

The summer of Ryan's eighth year, we sat around the kitchen table, Gazetteers and Rand McNally's sprawled across the wood surface, trying to choose an unforgettable, yet manageable adventure to celebrate Ryan's birth. For whatever reason that I don't exactly recall, we chose Big Sky Country. The plan was to head east, see a long lost high school friend, camp in the Stillwater Valley, drive Going to the Sun Highway and circle back home through the Yak Valley, visiting that last, remote valley best described by Rick Bass in his book *Winter*. It was a great trip and so began an acknowledgment of a new family tradition - The Birthday Trip.

There was no real rhyme or reason to the how or why we chose a particular destination. Over the winter and spring months "somewhere" would pique our interest and Ry would write to chambers of commerce and state tourism boards. We would check the mail and after a few weeks, maps, pamphlets, and discount books would fill our mailbox. We would sit, plan, conspire, imagine and hit the road by mid-July. The first few trips following Montana were simple road journeys exploring the northwest states that we called home.

There was the "all things volcano" trip to eastern Oregon. We learned about lava tubes, hiked fields of obsidian, and were blown away by the unparalleled beauty of Crater Lake. The Priest Lake trip had us marveling at the late night moose visits to the campsite - large, foreboding bodies casually meandering between the cars and tents, while we sat holding our breaths hoping that we hadn't offended Bullwinkle.

After those three trips, it seemed like a good time to fly the friendly skies to our next destination. By this time Ry was 11 and I felt like it was high time he saw our nation's capital. Instead of flying directly into Dulles like normal human beings, we opted to head to Atlanta, see his grandparents and drive to D.C. via the Blue Ridge Parkway and Skyline Drive through the Shenandoah. I was eager for Ry to experience some traditional Southern places before they disappeared, with urbanites building second and third homes, "roughing it" in the Blue Ridge. We ate peach pie, listened to an impromptu bluegrass jam in some generous person's barn and logged 435 miles at 35 mph in a beat up rental car with squishy suspension. Once we got to D.C., we eagerly ditched the car and embraced all that the Metro had to offer and headed into the city.

The Mall is a magical place. There is free entry to museum upon museum, monuments that bring tears to your eyes and a Crayola box collection of nationalities and languages floating about that define the melting pot of humanity. As luck would have it, Ry and I were there when the Folk Music Festival was in full swing. Ry's musical self perked up with each concert venue we enjoyed, as we ducked in and out of the Smithsonian to escape the heat and discover new national treasures. It was a glorious trip that reconnected us to family, heritage, dear friends and patriotic pride for this country we call home. Not to mention the Hare Krishna's that decided to have a peace rally on the fourth of July. Bless their hearts.

After returning from D.C., Ry and I decided that we would begin an every other year approach. Every other year we would fly to our destination, but continue exploring our home spaces the opposing years.

On the heels of our Washington trip, the Redwoods seemed like the next natural exploration. I had a race in the Columbia River Gorge and Ry and I decided to head to California directly afterward. After a quick stop to visit with friends in Portland, we hit Highway 101 and began our eye candy drive down the Oregon coast. How does one describe the natural beauties of the Pacific coastline? If you pay attention, it has a strength and fury that leaves you breathless. Ry and I slowly worked our way south, in no particular hurry, enjoying all that the drive had to offer.

The Redwood forest is a magical space and leaves anyone with introspection at a loss for words. Ry and I walked through hobbit-esque trails, communing with Ent-like stately trees, here before the American Revolution, straining impossibly high above the forest floor, creating a canopy of long ago lost histories. It was a wonderful trip - Roosevelt Elk, shamrock covered forest floors, Fern Canyon, Corkscrew tree, Avenue of the Giants and the now lost to us, Pioneer Cabin Tree.

The next year we had the good fortune to go abroad. I really wanted Ry to experience other parts of the world. The United States and Canada, for that matter, are large insular, homogenous continental spaces. I was eager for my son to understand how other citizens of the world lived and interacted, a chance to get away from the censored and sanitized American view of Europe. After a fair amount of research, we decided on the Netherlands. Travelling with a special needs child can be daunting, challenging and in most cases extremely stressful. When things go sideways, and they often do, you worry about how others will view the situation. Will you be safe? Therefore the ability to clearly communicate is a top priority. The Netherlands, specifically Amsterdam, provided a comfortably English speaking country, which was paramount, and they loved their bikes, which was delightful. We were all in. With the support of a dear friend and my parents, Ry, my nephew Christopher and I hopped the pond and headed to Europe.

I'm not quite sure how anyone can go to Europe and not have a jaw dropping, "that's remarkable" moment. We saw the house where Anne Frank hid, a pipe organ that Mozart played, Van Gogh after Van Gogh, cruised canal after canal and biked 15k to the North Sea on bike roads, not bike lanes. And of course, my wunderkind began to tease out Dutch within days. It was a glorious adventure that left us hungry for more trips abroad.

On the heels of Amsterdam, Ry and I thought it would be great to travel to Banff. I had been there years ago with his father, but Ry had never seen the splendor of the Canadian Rockies. We stayed in Banff Village for a couple of days, hiking and biking around the general area, Ry soon discovering that his mom was more than a little bit concerned about the abundant bear population. From there we camped at the base of the Lake Louise area, hiked to the Plain of the Six Glaciers Tea House and had biscuits and tea. It was there that I had one of those "*a-ha!*" moments. Ry and I were sitting there, enjoying our snack when it dawned on me that we were at the same table that his father and I had been at twenty years earlier. As I sat there, distractedly listening to what Ry was saying, I silently told Lee that he would have been so proud of this young man sitting across from me.

One evening, winter of 2014, I was watching 60 Minutes, and they were featuring the Basílica de la Sagrada Família, Gaudí's architectural masterpiece. At this time Ry had become interested in architecture and drafting. He had just completed a scale drawing of an elementary school design that he presented Ron Cowan, Bellingham School District's Executive Director of Facilities. As I watched the segment on *60 Minutes*, it was there and then that I decided that Spain was on our bucket list. So once again, scrimping like crazy and with the generous support of my parents and dear friend, Ry, Chris and I hopped on planes and headed to the third largest country in the E.U.

Spain lived up to expectations and then some. We arrived
in Barcelona and hit the ground running. The Basílica de la
Sagrada Família was awe-inspiring and Montjuïc provided
stunning views of the city and Mediterranean Sea. The
walk down the hill from Montjuïc had us casually strolling
past the Olympic Stadium and Palau de Catalunya. From
Barcelona we caught a high-speed train to Madrid. Madrid,
the nation's capital, was an urbanite's delight. We stayed
one block from both the Gran Vía, Madrid's version of
Times Square, and the Royal Palace. We toured the palace,
the Prado, El Rastro and took a day trip to Toledo, to walk
cobblestone streets and tour its world famous cathedral.
Our last destination was Granada - we were eager to walk
the grounds of the Alhambra. As we climbed out of the
desert-like valley floor through increasingly lush
woodlands to reach the fortress, the importance of water
to these Moorish peoples was not lost on us.

The Alhambra is a masterpiece of design. It is hard to
articulate the intricate Arabic wood and tile work that
defines the inner sanctum of this sprawling structure.
Surrounding the building are labyrinths of jeweled gardens
cultivated around an array of reflecting pools and
aqueducts carrying crystal clear water throughout the
grounds. The gurgling sound of water was in steady

competition with raucous birdcalls and noisy tourists. It was a juxtaposition of sensory input as I tried to imagine life there in the 13th century. Our last little adventure in Andalusia was passing through the Muslim gates and exploring that district of Granada. It was here that we were flooded with the smells of hookah pipes, spices and citrus sitting under the shade of orange trees, drinking cold sangria while listening to lost souls bang out Bob Dylan on their tired guitars.

As we bid farewell to this colorful, college town, we hopped aboard one last high-speed Renfe train bound for Barcelona passing orchards of olive trees at 300 kph. As luck would have it, our party was seated with an elderly Spanish woman who spoke not a lick of English. For five exhausting hours she spoke a non-stop stream of stories at us not caring one bit whether would or could not participate in the fabric of her conversation. It left my brain tired, my heart full and planted a well-earned smile on all of our faces.

As we continue to plan more birthday trips, I am thankful that Ry's autism does not prevent our adventuring. He does not suffer from sensory overload. In fact, he relishes the chaos associated with airports and train stations. His obsession with maps has gotten us out of more than a few missteps while traveling in other cities, and his utter fascination with history and science has allowed us to geek out in museums, and given me carte blanche to stop at roadside historical markers without his complaint. I think we are perfectly matched travel companions.

Baby Steps

I do not know a single parent with an autistic child that would not make a deal with the devil to understand the inner processing machinations of their little one's mind. I remember very early- on trying to understand what was coursing through Ryan's head. He could stare a hole right through the center of my heart, disconnected, but intensely focused. He also had repetitive behaviors that, on the surface, had no rhyme or reason as far as I could ascertain.

One fall evening, he must have been fifteen to sixteen months old, Ry, crawling, noticed his shadow on the wall. His body was backlit by the light from the ceiling fan and he was fascinated. He crawled up to his shadowed self, curious, reaching out and touching the wall. For the better part of thirty minutes my diapered, infant son chased and played with his shadow - back and forth, to and fro, exploring and maybe playing a game. On first blush, after my utter delight, I was astonished with his depth of focus. It became unnerving and I began to worry and question. In retrospect, I think most itty-bitties would have grown tired after a few minutes, but not my Ry. I began to wonder what could capture his attention so intently for such a relatively long span of time.

As I mentioned before, by two, he would sit in his sandbox and pour sand from measuring cup to measuring cup, again and again, mesmerized by the falling silica crystals reflecting the evening light. He didn't smile, laugh or "play" with the sand, he simply watched it spill out of the cups, cascading into the box. The scientist in me wondered if he was attracted to the refraction of sun rays, colors glinting off the geometric cubes of glass. The mother in me wondered if he was soothing himself from a world he found too chaotic and threatening. And then, there was the acknowledgment that maybe, just maybe (fingers crossed), he was having fun. I asked him more than once: "What? Why the sand?" And he simply replied, "*I do not know.*" It was his comfort zone, his pleasure and I was not going to get in the way of that.

Then there were the repetitive hand movements around his face, on the forehead, just outside of his visual periphery. Once again, no breadcrumbs to lead me to an answer - c'mon Ry, I just need a clue or two. I was a little desperate to have answers, what parent wouldn't? But again, I was left with very little.

When Ry was three, as we traversed campus one afternoon, leaving the Child Development Center and heading to my office, he kept repeating the letters "x" and "t". As I held his hand, lost in my reverie of a beautiful spring day, I realized that Ry was focused on the sidewalk. If we walked parallel to the lines, he said "t". If we walked obliquely to the lines, he said "x". And sure as shooting, the lines created the letters "t" and "x". It was at that point I knew that I had to get outta of my 'Kim' head space, get very creative and find a way to put my brain into Ry space - not an easy task. And so began my hyper-vigilant observation of Ry's interactions with his environment, trying to bridge the gap.

As he aged, his relationship with the surrounding world shifted and changed. He was fascinated with Coke machines, pushing the buttons over and over again. He loved riding in the elevator, staring intently as the floor lights blinked on and off as we rode up and down, down and up, he thrilled with the experience. If I needed to get work done around the house or in the garden, and he wouldn't nap, the next best entertainment was the pantry. Ry would stand or sit in front of the food pantry reading nutrition labels for hours. It was part of his hyperlexia and a little bit of a fixation, but he was happy and pleased with himself. The nutritionist in me loved it, the widow in me breathed a sigh of relief, but the mama in me regulated it so that Ry didn't spend his days in my kitchen cabinets, isolated from social construct and being baby-sat via General Foods and Beatrice.

Over time it became easier for me to make assumptions about his behaviors because I was armed with a raft of neurodevelopmental terms. In elementary school, during recess, Ry would stand next to the Newcomb stand, ear against the pipe, banging away. What was he doing? I hadn't a clue. What did I think he was doing? Satisfying his perfect pitch self, shutting out the bedlam of noises on the playground or engaging in self-stimulating behavior?

Ry also spent a lot of time scripting, repeating over and over again, the lyrics or chord progression of a song, a paragraph in a book, or a phrase he heard on the evening news. I would listen to him, quietly whispering the words over and over again. I have heard autism experts refer to it as a fixation, a way to calm the nervous system. When I have asked Ry, he simply shrugged, me thinking that it either sounds good to his ear, he is trying to sort out the information or that he feels compelled. But one evening, during his seventh year, while I was cooking dinner, I heard him repeating phrases to himself. "Ry, whatcha' talking about?" Ry, " *I am thinking about copyright law.*" Me,

"Why are you repeating those words over and over again?"
Ry, " *learning*." And there you have it. After seventeen
years, I finally got a definitive answer for his scripting! He
is just trying to make sense of the convolutions and
information in his life.

I find it interesting that the longer I am a parent of an
autistic child, the less I know about the disorder. The
complexity is daunting - a mosaic of curious subtleties and
behaviors, every autistic is different. I think I can compare
an initial diagnosis of autism to the five stages of grief:

First, there is fear. Why is my infant child struggling with
simple tasks? Not pointing to objects he wants, making
very little eye contact, not wanting to be held or shrinking
away from other children or unfamiliar spaces and sounds,
perhaps rocking incessantly, unusual fixations, and
volcanic tantrums.

Second, shock and denial! What do you mean my child
isn't "okay"? What does that mean - autism? Will he have a
normal life? This cannot be true! Are you sure? Every
parent of a newly diagnosed child has had this shell-
shocked experience. There is not a single parent on this

beautiful Earth that wants to hear that their child has a non-curative medical problem.

Third, information overload! Research, research, and web search. I always tell my college students that there is a difference between research and a web search. Parents look for confirmation. Does my beautiful child really fit the criteria for autism? Perhaps it is a mistake. What can I do to fix this problem? Omega-3 fatty acids, probiotics, gluten-free diets, the list goes on and on. There is a plethora of really bad websites that take advantage of the fear gripped by the families of this new diagnosis In some cases, these sites are downright dangerous, suggesting that they can cure autism through dangerous procedures like unnecessary chelation or avoiding vaccinations.

Fourth, blame! What caused my son's autism! If you go online, there are more than a few conspiracy theorists, uninformed, anecdotal individuals that will blame vaccines for the rise of autism. It does not matter that there is not one shred of empirical evidence to support their claims. Desperate and uninformed parents are just looking for causality. Unfortunately, they are hitting the bull's eye on the wrong target. Autism is genetic, perhaps inheritable and it's kind of hard to change your familial DNA or a spontaneous shift in nucleotides.

And lastly, there is acceptance. It may take days, weeks, and months to get to this place. Now what? At this stage parents have begun to hunker down for the long haul - early interventions, intakes, therapies, I.E.Ps, medications, exhaustion and a celebration that they are finally equipped to begin the heavy lifting to help their child.

I accepted Ry's diagnosis fourteen years ago, but still struggle with the outcome. I have days when my levels of frustration rise. Why? I am afraid of his future, plain and simple. I want Ry to have a life independent of me. I do not need to be independent of him. As far as I am concerned, he can live with me for forever. But I know he wants to lead his own life and also, I am not going to live forever. Ry needs to learn to take care of Ry and I am not sure that he is capable, ergo, fear. Only time will tell.

Legal-ease

It took me five pregnancies and thirty-four years to see Ryan for the very first time. It's not that I struggled in becoming pregnant; I just wasn't very gifted at staying pregnant. My first three pregnancies ended in early miscarriages. It was sad and disappointing, but did not leave me with knee-buckling grief and I soldiered on without too much difficulty. The fourth pregnancy was fully into the third trimester when something went horribly wrong and I lost Galen Patrick. After that devastating loss, I wasn't sure I had the stripes to give it one more try. I'm certain that it had never crossed my mind that I could or would be incapable of having a child. I think that childbearing is something that every young woman assumes will and can happen with regularity and ease if she desires it. It isn't until you are in my or a similar situation that you begin to wonder why no one ever explained to you that having a child isn't a reproductive guarantee and things won't always go as planned.

After a few months of heavy grieving and lots of conversations with myself, my hubby and the doctor, Lee and I decided to try one last time. I had just turned the corner on 34 and was feeling the tick tock of my biological clock and the older age of my husband. And truth be told, my heart couldn't take too much more sadness surrounding the loss of another pregnancy. Within a couple of months of trying, I was pregnant again, thrilled, but frightened of the uncertainty of the next forty weeks. I did everything by the book, which in itself was a challenge for me and Ry's pregnancy mostly went off without a hitch. He was even kind enough to have hiccups 24 hours a day, every day, throughout the last trimester...just a little reminder to me that he was okay.

There are so many instances of intimacy between partners expecting a child. Who will they look like? Will she have your eyes: will he have your smile and laugh? Maybe he will love the cello; perhaps she will master the perfect jump shot. We better start saving for college, now! It goes on and on. It is an exercise in hope, love and futures and it never occurs to anyone that this imagined white picket fence world may not take shape. My situation was no different. Lee and I talked about the wonderful life our son would have and how fabulous it was going to be to share our experiences with this much wanted and loved child.

It was an absolute given that Ryan would be an amazing athlete. His father was a decorated national champion gymnast and I was a fairly dedicated tomboy that enjoyed a palette of athletic endeavors. Lee and I had received higher education graduate degrees and knew Ryan would cruise through his academic pursuits without much difficulty. All in all, we were confident that this baby was going to be the perfect amalgamation of our genetic bits and pieces. Nothing could have been further from the truth. Ryan was very little of what Lee and I had imagined but everything that found us totally and crazily in love with this little boy.

As Ry grew older, I dedicated myself to learning more about his complexly disordered self...trying to find the right combination of therapies, medications, support and activities that would help Ry meet his fullest potential. There was not a chance that he would not receive the best care that I could find for him. During this time, regardless of the usual setbacks, I always firmly hoped (and maybe believed) that Ryan, like most other children, would live an independent life away from me as he approached young adulthood. After his traumatic brain injury, I slowly and painfully came to the realization that this was probably not going to happen according to a predictable timeline and it took the wind right out of my sails. I was deeply saddened because I knew he would not have the future we had worked so hard for or the future he wanted for himself. I wasn't really sure what it all meant, but I did know that I had to get busy reimagining what life would be like after he graduated from high school.

When a child turns eighteen, their legal status changes. They are of the age of majority and can act independently of their parents. They are able to enter into contracts freely, acquire credit cards, own property, discuss medical procedures, join the military - basically act on their own behalf, independent of their parent's best wishes or in many cases, demands. When Ry turned eighteen, he would be like any other young adult, except that he wasn't any other young adult.

My son has very little concept of money. I can feel the eye roll of many parents thinking that their seventeen year old still hasn't mastered a budget or self control around spending. That's not what I mean. Ryan, conceptually, doesn't understand money. He can spend it, he can earn it (sort of) but it is meaningless and intangible to him - think Monopoly money. He can't recognize that there are financial limits and people have to earn money before they spend it, that there is inherent value to currency or that he should keep his money safe. More than a few times, I have found ten and twenty dollars bills littering the floor of his bedroom, him not really caring about the value of that printed paper. The first thing that I wanted to do was to figure out how to protect him financially. I did not want someone to take advantage of him - internet scams, bogus telemarketing, or unscrupulous sales people seeing him as an easy mark. The only way I could prevent that was to get control over his monies.

There are two significant avenues that parents with special needs children can explore to protect finances. One is to create a special needs third party irrevocable trust. It gives the trustee (me) and the backup trustee (a trusted family friend) control over spending and it does not interfere with qualifying for and receiving the minimal social security disability benefits. A third party trust helps to insure a financial future for a child that may not have the ability to support them self. It allows parents and family to contribute to the financial welfare of the individual without repercussion.

The second pathway is for the parent to become the guardian of the estate. This means that the parent is in full control of the adult child's money, has to report annually to the courts and it protects the adult child from entering into or being responsible for financial contracts if someone is trying to take advantage.

Once I had control over his money, it was time to get control over him. Ry has been a long-standing patient at the local children's hospital. His medical condition is more complex than just autism and requires constant care. Ry is not capable of making informed medical decisions for himself. Actually, that isn't accurate. Ry is not able to understand the implications of making medical decisions and that complicates things. When he turns eighteen, I have no legal standing to be part of the conversation with his doctors. Ryan can usurp my voice in the conversation and there is very little that the doctor or I can do about that. It is the law and it is his right. The only avenue available in order for the parent to be allowed involvement is to be awarded guardianship of the person. Guardian of the person allows me to continue to act on behalf of Ry's best interest. It gives me legal permission to continue as an active participant in Ry's medical and daily care.

So, with all of that knowledge in mind, I began the eight month legal process of creating a trust and petitioning the court to be awarded guardianship over my soon to be legal adult son. Eighteen years ago when I was pregnant with

Ryan, it never crossed my mind that my child would have a life of medical difficulty or developmental disability. I never once considered that I would have to be granted legal authority to parent him into adulthood, but here I was doing just that.

As I sat in the courtroom, listening to my lawyer speak to the judge, a feeling of sadness and general relief flowed over me. Sad that I had to be there asking to continue in my role as guardian, relief that the process was coming to a close and that I was moving past another parenting hurdle. As the judge listened to my lawyer advocate for Guardianship, David told the judge that I was in the courtroom. The judge turned to me and asked, "*How is your son*"? Sitting there, I took a deep breath, a smile erupted from my face and I simply said, "*He is amazing*". Guardianship granted! Flooded with relief, I gave myself a small fist pump, exited the courtroom and called my parents with the news.

As Ryan ages, changes, matures and develops, I have the ability to pull back and give him more freedoms, fingers crossed that I will morph into a limited guardianship role over time. It is something he wishes and something I hope for. In the meantime, I am converting my garage into a studio apartment.

Inclusion

It's a Saturday morning and Ry is trying to configure his
computer to integrate with my older flat screen television.
There is a potpourri of computer and audio cables strewn
across the surface of the mule trunk and the TV, pulled
forward, is precariously balanced near the edge. It is not
the first time he has messed around with that set up, and I
know it won't be the last. I wasn't really curious or
concerned about his activity, I had long since gotten past
that stressor, but more interested in engaging him in
conversation.

As I walk into the family room, I see that he has an
episode of *Sesame Street* on his computer screen. In the last
few months Ry has developed a real love for the show. I
know he is seventeen, but his emotional development is
way behind the curve. I'm not entirely clear why he is
enamored with the show, but I suspect that he feels safe, is
learning about emotions and enjoys the lessons that they
have about friendship. As much as I would love for Ry to
catch up with his contemporaries, he has his own timeline
and there is no use pushing him to go somewhere,
sometime, if he is not ready.

Once he gets the television/computer issue worked out, he slowly settles on the couch and watches. As I cut through the room, I notice that he is watching the debut of Julia, *Sesame Street*'s newly created autistic Muppet. I stop and watch. *Sesame Street* is doing a remarkable job of introducing this character, but more to the point, introducing children to the differences of autism. The dialogue between the characters is heartfelt and the way in which they lovingly explain symptoms like sensory overload, lack of eye contact and withdrawal is a marvel. In that instance I feel a moment of hopefulness that children like Ryan will be more accepted by their peers and bullied less.

At the conclusion of the show, I ask, "*Ry, how do you feel about Julia?*" Ry responds, "*It feels amazing that shows like* Sesame Street *are finally addressing autism! If I could meet one person, it would be Miss Gordon, although at present we may live too far away from each other, because Julia, the character which she plays had a big impact on my life!*" And at seventeen years of age, my son finally has a character that looks, acts and sounds like him and he is tickled pink. In a single broad stroke, my son felt like he was part of the conversation and had been validated, but it has not always been that way.

When Ryan was a small child I was at my wit's end trying to decide how best to integrate and include him with his peers. He was being mainstreamed by the school district, but that was only a small percentage of a child's social currency. I mentioned in an earlier chapter that some parents had once asked what was wrong with Ry when he was three years old. I left that experience knowing that my uphill climb to inclusion was double edged and I would have to battle bias from parents and children.

The children in Ry's elementary school were nice to him, delightful in fact, and he was never really bullied there. There was a small group of girls, four or five of them, that I endearingly called the hens. They would collect Ryan, take him onto the playground and encourage him to tag along. They were sweet, kind and caring, but Ry never got invited to their birthday parties or to their homes after school. It never occurred to any one that Ry could be someone's friend. The children were more than willing to be with Ry at school, but once the last bell rang for the day, Ry was left without friends and headed home to his solitary world. I found no fault in them; it was just the reality of my child's circumstances.

[Added by Ryan Cunningham]

Being solitary is a very common circumstance for people with autism. Nonetheless, Ryan feels very included and, almost always, his growth as a person is valued and cherished, although there are some faults. Ryan believes that autistics should be treated equally compared to those who are neurotypical or have neurological disorders other than autism.

[End section added by Ryan Cunningham]

In turn, I never had big birthday parties for him, inviting his classmates to the house. I was worried about the outcome. Worst case scenario, no one would show, feeling uncomfortable trying to negotiate Ry's differences. And then there was the issue of trying to understand how to make the party fun for all of the kids. I was out of my league. I did not know how to bridge the gap and I was more than a little bit protective of my son. And to compound the problem, Ry suffered anxiety around lots of children - it was too much for him and his nervous system couldn't manage.

By middle school the differences between Ry and his peers was an ever-widening gap. By this time Ry had developed some unusual tics (throat clearing, ear twisting), an odd way of communicating ('what if' questions galore) and had very little in common with his peers. Ry's extracurricular endeavors (Broadway musicals, complex computing and current events) were so far outside the realm of interests for tweens that Ry could not find his place among them. To complicate matters, Ry still had not mastered the give and take of a conversation. His need to report about his fixations left very little room for connection and impaired peer relationship development.

As I observed him being left behind socially, I felt relieved that Ry, because of his autism, had not internalized a sense of being ostracized. I was very wrong. One day at cross country practice, while we all stood around waiting for the coach, a sixth grader walked up to Ry (seventh grader) and began to make fun of him. Ry was standing there, towering over this boy, twisting his ear and shrinking before my eyes. My son was being bullied right in front of me! I decided to be watchful for just a moment more before intervening, hoping that perhaps another student would come to his rescue. In a flash, Ry looked at the kid and said, "*Are you so lame that you got to pick on the special needs kid?*" Mic drop! Ry shut that kid down by himself - way to go Ry! But wait, Ry identified himself as special needs and that made me incredibly sad. It was the first instance that I knew in which Ry had identified himself as different and I needed to be more vigilant. I also needed to find a way for Ryan to interact with his peers. He needed coaching, but he needed it from kids.

My dear friend Allison, parent to autistic twins and doctoral work in neuropsychology, came to the rescue. She had gotten her hands on curricula from UCLA that was designed to help boys like ours learn more about social construct and she brilliantly recruited some of her son's "friends" to coach our boys through the program. So every other Friday evening we would head to her house to hang out. The tweens would head to the rec room to work on social skills and the adults would gather in the kitchen and hope for the best. On most gatherings Ry would last about 30 minutes before he headed upstairs, eager to be apart form the other kids. The activities and social pressures were too much for him and he needed to decompress. Allison had a beautiful baby grand piano and Ry would serenade us while we waited for the rest of the kids to finish up. It was a great idea and was beautifully implemented, but Ryan was not ready and he continued to struggle.

As Ry headed towards high school, I began to vibrate - my nervousness of this transition apparent. Our creative school district boundaries had Ry going to a school that most of his long term peers would not be attending. These kids weren't his friends, but they did understand and advocate for him. I thought I might petition the district for a change in schools, but discovered his assigned school had a remarkable Special Education department and that was more important to me. Ry found a home in choir and cross-country, but he did not find friends. The gap was getting wider and he was not making meaningful connections with his peers. These young adults were interested in things Ry could not grasp. They were loud, melodramatic, YouTube and SnapChat watching teens and Ry could not relate. He was invited to join a group for Homecoming his freshman year, but it never happened again. I tried to create "playdates" but it was becoming apparent from parents and teens that it wasn't going to be a reality. And, the few times that Ry was invited somewhere, he balked and just wanted to be home.

As a parent, it can be heavy lifting to realize that you are your child's only friend. I am not complaining, far from it. I thoroughly enjoy all of my time with Ryan and feel it is a gift that I get to spend so much time with him; however, I want him to have a friend, a person other than me, that gets him! For now, I am planning prom night. Ry has decided that he wants to go and I want it to be a special night for him. I get the honor of being his dinner date and he will go to the dance alone, looking to connect with others in his own special way. Maybe someone will ask him to dance?

RYAN CUNNINGHAM
2808 PACIFIC ST
BELLINGHAM WA 98226-3538
USA

2017-05-08

ATTN SESAME STREET AND AUTISM
SESAME WORKSHOP
1 LINCOLN PLZ
NEW YORK NY 10023
USA

Dear Employees,

Your show, *Sesame Street*, has made me discover what autism really is. Were it not for the willingness of media organizations like you to reveal what it means to have autism, autistic people like me (and the famous Temple Grandin) would almost be dead. About 63% of 1,167 children studied in a national survey on bullying experiences of children on the autism spectrum were bullied.[1]

Without an autistic Muppet like Julia, we never can live the lives we dream of living. The presence of Julia as a character has taught me to accept that autism is just a change in someone's way of life, just like blindness, deafness, or muteness. Were it not for my autism, there would be no way for me to be such a great keyboardist and computer programmer. (I also have seizure disorder.)

I would so much like to say thank-you for your help.

Sincerely,

Ryan Cunningham

---

[1] Autism Speaks. "Combating Bullying." *Autism Speaks*, n.d. Web. 2017-05-08. https://www.autismspeaks.org/family-services/bullying.

A Swing and a Miss

After all that I had been through while raising Ryan, I firmly believed that my coat of armor was pretty thick, a little dented and rusted here and there, of course, but intact and impenetrable. Mostly that is, until I came to the realization that whether I liked it or not, my son was turning eighteen and almost simultaneously graduating from high school. My tension around these two events began brewing sometime in early December of the preceding year. Typical of me, I began to have increased difficulties with sleep and my general, generic sense of anxiety was percolating. As I mentioned in an earlier chapter, I initially believed that I was grieving the future I wanted for Ry versus the future he was going to live. In truth, I was flat out scared about the uncertainty of him fledging from our school district and reaching adulthood. A thousand thoughts raced through my head 24/7. What was he going to do next year? Would he be safe? Where would he be during the day? Who would monitor him while I was at work? What if there was an emergency? How would I get him off the computer and doing other things? How would he maintain connections in the community that we worked so hard to foster? The list went on and on and reeked of a mother's desperation to find a place at the next level for her special needs son.

Of course worrying was about zero percent effective or helpful and I needed to put that energy into positive motion. The first action item was to conference with his Special Education teacher, Mary. She had always been an enormous resource for me and I knew that she would have some ideas about how to move forward. Mary had mentioned and we had met with the Community Transitions team in the fall but Ry was balking at the idea. I'll get back to that in a moment.

Community Transitions seemed like the perfect lifeline for our family. When Ry was in ninth grade, with the encouragement of Mary, we had set his graduation date three years after his academic graduation. In other words, Ry was a member of the class of 2017, but we set his matriculation for 2020. By doing this, it allowed Ry to remain in the school district until he turned twenty-one. Enter Community Transitions. C.T. is a remarkable program that takes special needs students and prepares them for independent living. The program follows the school district calendar, is in a school-like setting and is centrally located in town - all stress reducing attributes.

In the mornings the students have a job coach and practice filling out applications, job shadow and work at various businesses throughout our community. The afternoons are dedicated to mastering independent living and building social skills. The program is well planned, brilliantly administered and I was super excited for Ry to head there in September. There was one small problem - he was flat out refusing.

His push back was not about the program itself, it was something far more sinister...at least in his mind. You see, Ry was going to be "graduating" in June and he would be walking across the stage and receiving his fake diploma just like every other student at his school; however, in order to enter Community Transitions, he couldn't receive his real diploma in the mail the following week... like every other student. In fact, he could not obtain his diploma until he graduated from that program. And here is where the problem began.

Ry wanted to be treated like his peers. He had done the heavy lifting; taking AP classes, End of Course exams, scads of homework, extracurricular activities, just like everyone else. But he wasn't being treated just like everyone else. For him, that was intolerable, unconscionable and objectionable and I heard about it from him for weeks. My task was to find a solution that he felt good about and would still allow him entry into Community Transitions the following school year.

I suggested that we buy a frame for his diploma and leave it at his high school's main office. The staff agreed to let him come by any time and look at it. Nope, that wasn't acceptable. How about we scan it, frame the scanned version and bring that home? Again, it wasn't the same as the real thing. After weeks and weeks of trying and beginning to feel defeated and quite desperate, graduation loomed and I had no idea of my next course of action. Running out of time and surrendering, I decided that my only course of action was to flex my guardianship muscles and inform both the school and Ry that the diploma was to remain at school and that was my final decision. Feeling empowered and a little bit bullish, I was prepared to say "No".

And so, on a beautiful Saturday morning I proudly watched Ry graduate with all of his peers; parents and grandparents, armed with cameras and bouquets, filled the gymnasium. Small children cried, fidgeted and whispered loudly, getting *'the look'* from moms and dads. Student speakers, trying to be grown up, testing allowable phrases, spoke to their class about bright futures and making differences in the world. It was a high school graduation like any other across the nation and from years past, traditions never wavering. And when all was said and done, Ry never asked about his diploma - not a peep, word, or argument. Months of worry, manipulation, conspiring and planning were for naught. Once again, those hours of lost sleep and worrying, were unnecessary.

There are a lot of personality traits and life skills that have helped me parent Ry. Being tenacious and competitive gave me the strength to soldier on and not give up. Having a strong academic background gave me the skills to educate myself about his disability and to be a strong advocate. Being an athlete and physically strong provided me the ability to keep him safe during his worst behavioral outbursts, but having a sense of humor allowed me (and him) to survive both of us.

A Hole In My Heart

My brother in-law, Dan, not married to any blood relation, or a blood relation of mine, was diagnosed with end stage pancreatic cancer in early May. He was part of a very complex and layered Washington family that welcomed me as their own without question or hesitation before the turn of the century. When I heard the diagnosis from Dan's doctor, one of my primary concerns was how this life development would impact Ryan. In his short eighteen years of life, he had already experienced titanic loss and I was concerned that this new diagnosis and inevitable death would dredge up sadness or abandonment issues with regard to his own father's illness. I parked that in the back of my mind, kept a watchful eye on my son and focused my energy on Dan and his wife.

Dan was married to my late husband's twin, Lyn. She, in recent years, developing and suffering from dementia, had fundamentally left us, but held onto her sweet constitution. She struggled remembering any of us with consistency…deferring to Dan almost exclusively to help her make simple daily decisions…oftentimes referring to him as her son, Brad, and only recognizing Ry as the piano player - not remembering that he was Lee's son or even that she had a brother.

For weeks, that stretched into months and then a couple of years, Ry and I had a weekly standing dinner date with Dan and Lyn or would visit them at their home. It was an opportunity to spend time with them as Lyn began her slow decline and it gave Dan some respite from the heavy lifting of 24/7 caretaking. Many of their friends had pulled back as it became more and more difficult to navigate the changes and rigid routines that dominated their household. Ry would frequently sit down at the keyboard in the corner of the living room and happily play Broadway musicals for an hour or two, Lyn listening with a smile on her face, Dan and I discussing sports and politics while watching baseball, golf or CNN with the sound off. Over time we fell into an easy Sunday evening rhythm, which from an outsiders perspective, might best be described as strange, but the true nature of our relationship.

During the winter and early spring the visits began to change shape. Lyn's anxiety of unfamiliar places was making it difficult for us to meet publicly for dinner and, therefore, we were relegated to short afternoon visits at their house. The consistency of the visits was tapering off and Ry and I would have periods of two to three weeks without seeing them, but continuing to check in by phone to make sure things had not gotten really bad for Lyn or Dan, for that matter.

In late March or April, after a three week hiatus, I finally made time to spend an afternoon with them. On this particular visit Ry, displaying the normalcy of adolescence, opted out and decided he'd rather stay home and be on his computer instead of visiting his aunt and uncle. Knocking on their door, Dan opened it and I immediately thought, "*What in the hell is going on here*"? In a matter of weeks, my brother-in-law, someone best described as strong and robust, had easily lost 25 pounds. Instantly, I knew he was very sick and thus began my journey - helping him die.

The first order of business was to find a safe place for Lyn so that he could receive treatment. In Dan's mind, he believed he had a simple blockage or growth in his colon that could be addressed with surgery. He had been suffering from alternating constipation and diarrhea for a number of weeks and his anorexia and weight loss were beginning to concern him. This was a man that never missed a meal.

As he was explaining all of this to me, I sat, bewildered, asking myself. "Why hadn't he gone to the doctor sooner? Why hadn't he called, reached out, asked for help?" Simple answer, he needed to find a respite situation for Lyn first before acting in his best interest. Shaking my head, I explained that I could have sat with her while he was at the doctor and I was quickly rebuffed. For Dan, there was only one path and solution by which he would seek treatment and that was the end of the discussion. Fair enough, I knew better than to argue with him.

As Lyn was temporarily ensconced in a local memory care facility, Dan was able to get an appointment with his general doc and get a CT scan ordered. In a few days, he was referred to the local cancer center and had a scheduled appointment with an oncologist. As he was explaining all of this to me, I had a few thoughts course through my head:

-He is alone in this journey. Dan didn't have friends. All of his social currency came from Lyn's friends and they had slowly pulled back in the past year.

-He needs help. To say that my life is complicated would be an understatement. Raising Ry, working full-time, managing a home and trying to have a little "me" time had become an art form. I was reluctant to upset that apple cart. But Dan was family and there was no one else.

-How sick is he? I did not think he had a simple blockage and suspected that something else was afoot, the obvious candidate was lung cancer. Dan had been a heavy smoker most of his life.

As we talked about his appointment, I offered to go with him to take notes, advocate and to just keep him company. He welcomed my offer and we were to meet at the cancer center in a few days.

When Ry got home from school that day. I explained to him that Uncle Dan was sick, probably had cancer, would need treatment and we were going to help. Ry listened, asked a few questions and then explained how sorry he was for Dan. He thought it would be great for us to visit Lyn at the memory care facility and play piano for her in the commons area - hoping to make her feel more at home and eagerly wanting to get his hands on their baby grand piano. And so my focus split…organizing visits to Lyn and supporting Dan.

I am no stranger to cancer. Most of my family members have been diagnosed and survived a variety of cancers. I lost my husband to lung cancer when I was 39 and one of my best friends, Salma, to multiple myeloma a few years later. I had been there with them during doctor and emergency room visits, cleaned vomit, organized medication schedules, held hands as they were dying, while loving, hugging, and crying together. These were the things I knew how to do, but I found myself in unfamiliar territory with Dan.

Dan was not an open person. He was very reserved, private, rigid and had a healthy case of obsessive-compulsive disorder, coupled with anxiety. So, as I sat with him in the oncology waiting room, I wondered how I would comfort and support him as he was getting news, what I perceived as bad news, from the doc. As we sat and listened, I moved from across the room, sat beside him and simply asked him, "*Are you okay?*" I knew of nothing else to do or offer - what do you say when someone is being told that if things go well, they have six months to live.

After the appointment, walking out to the car, I gave him a hug and told him I would be there for him - he was not gonna go it alone. He thanked me, said he was fine and would talk with me in a few days.

In the meantime, I had gotten permission from Lyn's memory care facility for Ry to play piano for the residents the following Sunday. After a phone call to Dan, the three of us carted ourselves off to Lyn's facility to enjoy an afternoon of piano, compliments of Ryan... or so I thought.

Did you know that there are copyright rules for music? Did you know that you cannot play certain musical pieces in public without permissions or a license from the publisher? No? Well, neither did I! As Ry cued up to the piano, he began to vigorously twist his ear - landmark indicator of stress. But for the life of me, I could not understand why he was upset. He had publicly performed numerous times and never once balked at the idea. Here we were, surrounded by elderly dementia patients who were not paying him the slightest bit of attention, and Ry was becoming unglued. After a few minutes of quiet inquiry, I finally discovered the root of his anxiety and I was off to the races. I casually walked over to the front desk, asked if they had permissions for public performances. They said' *"Of course"* and Ryan, relieved, played for two hours. The residents and his aunt were out of their chairs dancing, singing, clapping and generally having a grand time and I believed Dan welcomed the distraction. Ryan was thoroughly pleased with himself and promised to come back in a few weeks - which he did.

The next few weeks were a whirlwind of activity. Ryan was finishing up his senior year and was participating in all things graduation, choir and Unified soccer. I was determined to make sure that Dan's diagnosis and subsequent care did not shadow Ryan's successes in and out of the classroom and I worked on capturing the normalcy of the moment. In the meantime, I was getting an accelerated education on Dan and Lyn's finances, was appointed Dan's Durable Power of Attorney and accompanied him to doctor's visits all while trying to close out my school year. It was a remarkably busy time and I'm not sure I could have managed it without Ryan's newly gained independence and Dan's sister, Nancy, temporarily putting her life on hold to help her brother.

During the last half of June, it was becoming painfully obvious that Dan had mere weeks left. He was continuing to lose weight at a precipitous rate, developed jaundice, and could no longer manage his pain. With his permission, no easy task, Nancy and I called Hospice and managed to get him the help he needed.

In the meantime, I was beginning to worry about Ryan. He had lost his father to cancer just before turning five and I was wondering how Dan's rapid decline was affecting him. Like most parents, I used time in the car or at the dinner table to check in and see how he was handling everything. True to Ry, he was worried about Dan, curious about Lyn's outcome, but accepted that this was a natural process and was happy that I was helping. If only I could have had that grounded sense of ease about the world at such a young age.

At the end of June, we had to move Dan into Hospice House. We were no longer able to keep him safe in the household and Nancy was bordering on exhaustion. During the last few days of Dan's life Ry, was away at a residential camp. At the time it felt like a blessing. I could totally focus on Dan and not feel like I needed to get home to Ry. One less thing on my plate, and one less thing to worry about.

Dan died the morning of July 6th. He went away quietly in his sleep, breathing gently slowing down to nothingness.

His body was ragged and exhausted and he fought valiantly to the end. As I headed home to get some much needed rest, I felt lost and out of sync. I wasn't really sure what was happening. I was grieving for sure, but I felt discombobulated. Then it struck me! I needed Ry just as much as he needed me. While he was away at summer camp, I was grappling with life and death. I walked into our home, void of his music, child-like energy and empathy and I felt an emptiness of spirit and a sadness of heart. My emotional compass was off adventuring and I wasn't sure which direction I was pointing.

It took a few weeks to get my feet back under me and reclaim summer, but even more time to find a place of quiet ease that would help me process the past few months.

I suppose if there were gifts in this entire experience, they would be the opportunity to talk more with Ry about his father's battle with cancer, becoming closer to Dan's Canada family and a deeper appreciation that every day is a gift to be unwrapped and cherished.

Parting Thoughts

I am sitting at my local Social Security Administration
office waiting to hear them call C32 on the intercom
(currently the reader board flashes C17) and I hunker
down in my chair for the long haul, computer in my lap,
surrendering and writing this final chapter. My son was
denied Social Security Insurance in October. The powers
that be, not entirely convinced that Ryan cannot be
employed in a meaningful fashion, decided that he was not
eligible for government assistance. Thus, I am cued up to
debate that point.

This is my sixth trip here in three months and I am
becoming well versed and simultaneously weary. My first
visit, since my husband's death ages ago, was to get Ry's
Survivor's Benefits extended for an additional year.
Although he turned eighteen in the summer, because he
was in a special program that extended his graduation
three additional years, he is eligible for one more year of
benefits and I was determined to make sure that Ry
received every advantage available to him. I filled out the
forms and he was granted reprieve for twelve more
months. That gave me a bit of breathing room while I

wrangled the vagaries of continued Social Security Insurance for him as he enters adulthood.

The second trip was to establish that, although he is eighteen, I continued to be his legally appointed guardian. Armed with court documents declaring that I am that person, the SSA office assured me that they would continue to send pertinent documents to me and not Ryan. Sadly, that didn't happen and now I had to remind them that I am still the custodian of Ryan's affairs.

Third trip, and now the security guard knew me by name. We exchanged the usual sarcastic repartee about the nature of the Social Security Office and its local color. I was there to collect the necessary forms for Social Security Insurance and to ask lots of questions. I was out of my league and did not have an experiential base to work from. So, I ask questions - a lot of questions.

The woman working with me was wonderful, informative, understanding and gave me oodles of helpful information and pamphlets. I left feeling hopeful, mildly empowered and believing that I might be able to get Ry covered in the next few months.

Next visit was the intake interview with Ry, an SSA representative handling our case and me. She asked lots of questions of both Ry and me while filling out prerequisite forms. Me, nervous, trying best to explain the degree of Ryan's difficulties, all this while Ry sitting beside me having to hear that information and twisting his ears like crazy. It was an opportunity for Ryan and me to discuss the role of advocacy and my glass half full attitude. But I readily admitted that it didn't feel good for me to have these conversations in his presence. He agreed that it was difficult but necessary and I left learning more from him than he from me.

One month after finishing the intake, we received a letter and Ryan was denied Social Security Insurance. I wasn't prepared for the impact of that decision. As I read the report of denial, which was mailed to Ryan and not me, I slid to my kitchen floor and began to cry. Ry noticed my sadness asked what was happening. I simply handed him the letter and watched as he read. Crestfallen he looked at me and asked, "*Why is the government discriminating against me? I was born with disability and they do not believe me.*" As more sadness enveloped me, I thought what the hell does it take for him to be validated?

The next day, I collected myself and headed back to Social Security, and asked about the appeal process. Once again, I was treated with respect, dignity and kindness. The woman behind the glass partition gave me lots of info and more forms to complete. I took copious notes, that I promptly lost, and began the process of appealing the decision. In my appeal, I wrote a letter describing the extent of Ryan's disability. Try as I may to be clinical, I can't escape the emotional impact of recounting and contextualizing the extent of my child's disability. I want nothing more than for Ry to be heading to college, working part-time at Trader Joe's and dating some gal that thinks he is wonderful. But he isn't going to college yet, is not capable of employment and has no friends. So, here I am, forms in hand, with some of the supporting documentation, hopeful that I am doing everything correctly and that this time Ry will qualify. At the end of the week, fingers crossed, I again turn in all the forms.

When I think about the manner in which autism has impacted my son's life, it takes my breath away. The simplest interaction, like asking Ry, "*How are you doing?*" could stretch into a thirty second pregnant pause while Ry teased out all of the possible solutions to that question, trying to understand the intent of the question and to finally answer, "*Great!*" In the meantime, the questioner is left feeling uncomfortable or disinterested, having already mentally moved on, and Ry is left missing another chance at connection.

When I ask Ry how autism has impacted him, he states:

> *Some of the challenges I have had to overcome while living with autism were gravitational insecurity and not fitting in well with others. I overcame my gravitational insecurity by facing it first-hand.*
>
> *I am not sure how I felt about overcoming the challenge of gravitational insecurity and I believe I am still not yet completely fitting in with other people and that is hard for me.*

No one has ever questioned whether or not Ry has disability. I have long since learned not to be upset by people staring as we walk down a sidewalk, eat out at a restaurant or go for a hike. It used to frustrate and saddened me - protective and reactive simultaneously. Ry's carriage, voice volume, appearance and tics make it easy for the general public to understand that my son is different and they stare out of curiosity, not cruelty. But it still does not feel good.

I'm not sure that most people can understand the degree to which an autistic person wants to make social connections in their world or how overwhelming it is trying to do so. We, *neurotypicals*, stride through life, easily understanding subtle nuance and inference, never grasping the difficulty of a simple "*hello*". It is my hope that by writing this book, the reader will walk away from the experience with a better understanding of the uphill challenges of any person with special needs and the people that love and support them.

For now, I hold on to the notion that Ry, wanting to eventually live independently from me, will reach his goals and live the life he dreams of for himself. In the meantime, I will continue to foster and encourage him to find that path and to develop and master the life skills he needs to continue in the next chapter of his life.

Thanks for stopping by.

Love the Life You Live...
Kim and Ry